Daily Readings From
MY UTMOST
FOR HIS HIGHEST

Given to: _____

On: _____

By: _____

With this special message:

_____

_____

_____

DAILY READINGS FROM

MY
UTMOST
FOR HIS
HIGHEST

OSWALD
CHAMBERS

UPDATED EDITION

THOMAS NELSON PUBLISHERS
Nashville, Tennessee

ISBN 0-7852-8180-0

Library of Congress Cataloging in Publication Data is
available.

Library of Congress Card
93-85818

Printed in Singapore

1 2 3 4 5 6 7 8 — 98 97 96 95 94 93

MY
UTMOST
FOR HIS
HIGHEST

OSWALD
CHAMBERS

UPDATED EDITION

January

Let Us Keep to the Point

*My earnest expectation and hope
that in nothing I shall be ashamed.*
(Philippians 1:20)

It's as if Paul were saying, "My determined purpose is to be my utmost for His highest—my best for His glory."

Shut out every other thought and determine to be absolutely and entirely for Him and Him alone.

Will You Go Out Without Knowing?

He went out, not knowing where he was going. (Hebrews 11:8)

Let the attitude of your life be a continual willingness to "go out" in dependence upon God, and your life will have a sacred and inexpressible charm about it that is very satisfying to Jesus.

Learn to "go out" until you come to the point in your faith where there is nothing between yourself and God.

"Clouds and Darkness"

Clouds and darkness surround him.
(Psalm 97:2)

Once, the Bible was just so many words to us—"clouds and darkness"—then, suddenly, the words become spirit and life because Jesus re-speaks them to us when our circumstances make the words new. That is the way God speaks to us; not by visions and dreams, but by words.

JANUARY 3 _____

"Why Can I Not Follow You Now?"

Peter said to Him, "Lord, why can I not follow You now?" (John 13:37)

When God brings a time of waiting, and appears to be unresponsive, don't fill it with busyness, just wait.

Wait for God's timing and He will do it without any heartache or disappointment.

The Life of Power to Follow

Jesus answered him, "Where I am going you cannot follow Me now, but you shall follow Me afterward."
(John 13:36)

Build only on a Person, the Lord Jesus Christ and on the Spirit He gives.

There is now only One who directs the course of your life, the Lord Jesus Christ.

Worship

There he built an altar to the Lord and called on the name of the Lord.
(Genesis 12:8)

Whenever you get a blessing from God, give it back to Him as a love-gift.

Take time to meditate before God and offer the blessing back to Him in a deliberate act of worship.

Intimate with Jesus

Jesus said to him, "Have I been with you so long, and yet you have not known Me, Philip?" (John 14:9)

Once we get intimate with Jesus we are never lonely and we never lack for understanding or compassion.

The picture resulting from such a life is that of the strong, calm balance that our Lord gives to those who are intimate with Him.

Is My Sacrifice Living?

Abraham built an altar . . . and he bound Isaac his son and laid him on the altar. (Genesis 22:9)

It is of no value to God to give Him your life for death.

God never tells us to give things up just for the sake of giving them up, but He tells us to give them up for the sake of the only thing worth having—life with Himself.

Prayerful
Inner-Searching

*May your whole spirit, soul and
body be preserved blameless.*
(First Thessalonians 5:23)

It is only when we are protected
by God with the miraculous sacredness of the Holy Spirit that our
spirit, soul, and body can be preserved in pure uprightness until the
coming of Jesus—no longer condemned in God's sight.

We should more frequently allow
our minds to meditate on these
great, massive truths of God.

JANUARY 9

The Opened Sight

I now send you, to open their eyes . . . that they may receive forgiveness of sins. (Acts 26:17–18)

This verse is the greatest example of the true essence of the message of a disciple of Jesus Christ in all the New Testament.

Our job as workers for God is to open people's eyes so that they may turn themselves from darkness to light.

What My Obedience to God Costs Other People

*As they led Him away, they laid
hold of a certain man, Simon . . .
and on him they laid the cross that
he might bear it after Jesus.*
(Luke 23:26)

If we are in love with our Lord,
obedience does not cost us
anything—it is a delight.

Beware of the inclination to dictate to God what consequences you
would allow as a condition of your
obedience to Him.

Have You Ever Been Alone with God?

When they were alone, He explained all things to His disciples.
(Mark 4:34)

Jesus doesn't take us aside and explain things to us all the time; He explains things to us as we are able to understand them.

He will reveal numerous misplaced affections or desires—things over which we never thought He would have to get us alone.

Have You Ever Been Alone with God?

When He was alone . . . the twelve asked Him about the parable.
(Mark 4:10)

As you journey with God, the only thing He intends to be clear is the way He deals with your soul.

Jesus cannot teach us anything until we quiet all our intellectual questions and get alone with Him.

JANUARY 13 _____

Called by God

I heard the voice of the Lord, saying:
Whom shall I send, and who will go
for Us. Then I said, "Here am I!
Send me." (Isaiah 6:8)

The chosen ones are those who have come into a relationship with God through Jesus Christ and have had their spiritual condition changed and their ears opened.

Remove the thought from your mind of expecting God to come to force you or to plead with you.

Do You Walk in White?

*We were buried with Him . . . that
just as Christ was raised from the
dead . . . even so we also should
walk in newness of life.*
(Romans 6:4)

If there has never been this cru-
cial moment of change through
death, sanctification will never be
more than an elusive dream.

Once you truly realize this is
God's will, you will enter the process of sanctification as a natural response.

JANUARY 15 _____

The Voice of the Nature of God

I heard the voice of the Lord, saying:
"Whom shall I send, and who will
go for Us?" (Isaiah 6:8)

God providentially weaves the threads of His call through our lives, and only we can distinguish them.

To be brought to the place where we can hear the call of God is to be profoundly changed.

The Call of the Natural Life

When it pleased God . . . to reveal His son in me. (Galatians 1:15–16)

Service is the overflow which pours from a life filled with love and devotion.

When I receive His nature and hear His call, His divine voice resounds throughout His nature and mine and the two become one in service.

"It Is the Lord"

Thomas answered and said to Him,
"My Lord and my God."
(John 20:28)

The goal of the call of God is His satisfaction, not simply that we should do something *for* Him.

We are not sent to do battle for God, but to be used by God in His battles.

Vision and Darkness

When the sun was going down, a deep sleep fell upon Abram; and behold, horror and great darkness fell upon him. (Genesis 15:12)

The reason we are all being disciplined is so that we will know God is real.

As soon as God becomes real to us, people pale by comparison, becoming shadows of reality.

Are You Fresh for Everything?

Jesus answered and said to him, "Most assuredly, I say to you, unless one is born again, he cannot see the kingdom of God." (John 3:3)

Being born again from above is an enduring, perpetual, and eternal beginning.

Being born again provides a freshness all the time in thinking, talking, and living—a continual surprise of the life of God.

Recall What God Remembers

Thus says the Lord: "I remember . . . the kindness of your youth." (Jeremiah 2:2)

Am I so in love with Him that I take no thought for where He might lead me?

Or am I watching to see how much respect I get as I measure how much service I should give Him.

Am I Looking to God?

Look to Me, and be saved.
(Isaiah 45:22)

Our difficulties, our trials, and our worries about tomorrow all vanish when we look to God.

No matter how many things seem to be pressing in on you, be determined to push them aside and look to Him.

Transformed by Beholding

*We all, with unveiled face,
beholding as in a mirror the glory of
the Lord, are being transformed into
the same image.*
(Second Corinthians 3:18)

The most important rule for us is
to concentrate on keeping our
lives open to God.

The most difficult lesson of the
Christian life is learning how to continue "beholding as in a mirror the
glory of the Lord."

JANUARY 23

God's Overpowering Purpose

I have appeared to you for this purpose. (Acts 26:16)

The vision Paul had on the road to Damascus was not a passing emotional experience, but a vision that had very clear and emphatic directions for him.

When we are born again, if we are spiritual at all, we have visions of what Jesus wants us to be.

Leave Room for God

When it pleased God . . .
(Galatians 1:15)

No matter how well we may know God, the great lesson to learn is that He may break in at any minute.

We tend to overlook this element of surprise, yet God never works in any other way.

Look Again and Consecrate

If God so clothes the grass of the field . . . will He not much more clothe you? (Matthew 6:30)

Every time we lose ground in our fellowship with God, it is because we have disrespectfully thought that we knew better than Jesus Christ.

We have allowed "the cares of this world" to enter in (Matthew 13:22), while forgetting the "much more" of our heavenly Father.

Look Again and Think

Do not worry about your life.
(Matthew 6:25)

A warning which needs to be re-peated is that "the cares of this world and the deceitfulness of riches," and the lust for other things, will choke out the life of God in us (Matthew 13:22).

Our Lord says to be careful only about one thing—our relationship to Him.

How Could Someone So Persecute Jesus!

"Saul, Saul, why are you persecuting Me?" (Acts 26:14)

Whenever we are obstinate and self-willed and set on our own ambitions, we are hurting Jesus.

Whenever we rely on self-respect, we systematically disturb and grieve His Spirit.

JANUARY 28

How Could Someone be So Ignorant!

Who are You, Lord? (Acts 26:15)

I f the voice of God has come to you directly, you cannot mistake the intimate insistence with which it has spoken to you.

Have I been persecuting Jesus by an eager determination to serve Him in my own way?

JANUARY 29 —————————————

The Dilemma of Obedience

Samuel was afraid to tell Eli the vision. (First Samuel 3:15)

Chastening is more than a means of discipline—it is meant to bring me to the point of saying, "Speak Lord."

Never ask another person's advice about anything God makes you decide before Him.

Do You See Your Calling?

Separated to the gospel of God.
(Romans 1:1)

Personal holiness is an effect of redemption, not the cause of it. As long as our eyes are focused on our own personal holiness, we will never even get close to the full reality of redemption.

February

The Call of God

Christ did not send me to baptize,
but to preach the gospel.
(First Corinthians 1:17)

We are not commissioned to preach salvation or sanctification—we are commissioned to lift up Jesus Christ (see John 12:32).

Paul welcomed heartbreak, disillusionment, and tribulation for only one reason—these things kept him unmovable in his devotion to the gospel of God.

FEBRUARY 1 _____

The Compelling Force of the Call

Woe to me if I do not preach the gospel. (First Corinthians 9:16)

Everyone who is saved is called to testify to the fact of his salvation.

Once someone begins to hear the call of God, every ambition, every desire of life, and every outlook is completely blotted out and extinguished.

Becoming the "Filth of the World"

We have been made as the filth of the world. (First Corinthians 4:13)

We are too cautious and concerned about our own desires to allow ourselves to become the refuse or "filth of the world." A true servant of Jesus Christ is one who is willing to experience martyrdom for the reality of the gospel of God.

The Compelling Majesty of His Power

The love of Christ compels us.
(Second Corinthians 5:14)

The one thing that gripped and held Paul, to the exclusion of everything else, was the love of God.

Accept everything that happens as if it were happening to Him, whether we receive praise or blame, persecution or reward.

Are You Ready to Be Poured Out as an Offering?

If I am being poured out as a drink offering . . . I am glad and rejoice with you all. (Philippians 2:17)

It is one thing to follow God's way of service if you are regarded as a hero, but quite another thing if the road marked out for you by God requires becoming a "doormat."

Are you ready to be less than a mere drop in the bucket—to be so totally insignificant that no one remembers you even if they think of those you served?

FEBRUARY 5 _____

Are You Ready to Be Poured Out as an Offering?

I am already being poured out as a drink offering.
(Second Timothy 4:6)

Once you have experienced the crisis in your will, you will take no thought of the cost when it begins to affect you externally.

After you have gone through the fire, there will be nothing that will be able to trouble or depress you.

_____ **FEBRUARY 6**

Spiritual Dejection

*We were hoping that it was He who
was going to redeem Israel.*
(Luke 24:21)

We never realize that all the
time God is at work in our
everyday events and in the people
around us.

One of the most amazing revela-
tions of God comes to us when we
learn that it is in the everyday
things of life that we realize the
magnificent deity of Jesus Christ.

The Cost of Sanctification

May the God of peace Himself sanctify you completely.
(First Thessalonians 5:23)

The reason some of us have not entered into the experience of sanctification is that we have not realized the meaning of sanctification from God's perspective.

The resounding evidence of the Holy Spirit in a person's life is the unmistakable family likeness to Jesus and the freedom from everything which is not like Him.

Are You Exhausted Spiritually?

The everlasting God . . . neither faints nor is weary. (Isaiah 40:28)

Whether or not you experience exhaustion will depend on where you get your supplies.

Continually look back to the foundation of your love and affection and remember where your Source of power lies.

Is Your Ability to See God Blinded?

Lift up your eyes on high, and see who has created these things.
(Isaiah 40:26)

If your power to see has been blinded, don't look back on your own experiences, but look to God.

The power of visualization is what God gives a saint so that he can go beyond himself and be firmly placed into relationships he never before experienced.

Is Your Mind Stayed on God?

You will keep him in perfect peace,
whose mind is stayed on You,
because he trusts in You.
(Isaiah 26:3)

When you have thoughts and ideas that are worthy of credit to God, compare and associate them with all that happens in nature—the rising and the setting of the sun, . . . and the changing of the seasons.

Encourage yourself to remember and your affection for God will increase tenfold.

FEBRUARY 11 _____

Are You Listening to God?

You speak with us, and we will hear; but let not God speak with us, lest we die. (Exodus 20:19)

We don't consciously and deliberately disobey God—we simply don't listen to Him.

God has given His commands to us, but we pay no attention to them—not because of willful disobedience, but because we do not truly love and respect Him.

The Devotion of Hearing

Samuel answered, "Speak, for Your servant hears." (First Samuel 3:10)

A flower, a tree, or a servant of God may convey God's message to me.

If I have not developed and nurtured this devotion of hearing, I can only hear God's voice at certain times.

The Discipline of Hearing

Whatever I tell you in the dark,
speak in the light. (Matthew 10:27)

Pay attention when God puts you into darkness, and keep your mouth closed while you are there.

Don't talk to other people about being in the dark, don't read books to find out the reason for the darkness; just listen and obey.

"Am I My Brother's Keeper?"

None of us lives to himself.
(Romans 14:7)

If you allow physical selfishness, mental carelessness, moral insensitivity, or spiritual weakness, everyone in contact with you will suffer.

My life of service to God is the way I say "thank you" to Him for His inexpressibly wonderful salvation.

FEBRUARY 15 _____

The Inspiration of Spiritual Initiative

Arise from the dead.
(Ephesians 5:14)

When God sends His inspiration, it comes to us with such miraculous power that we are able to "arise from the dead" and do the impossible.

The remarkable thing about spiritual initiative is that the life and power comes after we "get up and get going."

Taking the Initiative Against Depression

Arise and eat. (First Kings 19:5)

If human beings were not capable of depression, we would have no capacity for happiness and exaltation.

When the Spirit of God leads us instinctively to do something, the moment we do it the depression is gone.

Taking the Initiative
Against Despair

Rise, let us be going.
(Matthew 26:46)

We will have times of despair caused by real events in our lives, and we will be unable to lift ourselves out of them.

If we are inspired by God the next thing to do is to trust Him absolutely and pray on the basis of His redemption.

Taking the Initiative Against Drudgery

Arise, shine. (Isaiah 60:1)

If we will arise and shine, drudgery will be divinely transformed.

In some cases the way a person does a task makes that work sanctified and holy forever.

Taking the Initiative Against Daydreaming

Arise, let us go from here.
(John 14:31)

When our purpose is to seek God and to discover His will for us, daydreaming is right and acceptable.

Allow Him to be the source of all your dreams, joys, and delights, and be careful to go and obey what He has said.

Do You Really Love Him?

"She has done a good work for Me."
(Mark 14:6)

Are you just sitting around day-dreaming about the greatness of His redemption, while neglecting all the things you could be doing for Him?

The issue is never of being of use, but of being of value to God Himself.

The Discipline of Spiritual Perseverance

Be still, and know that I am God.
(Psalm 46:10)

Perseverance is endurance combined with absolute assurance and certainty that what we are looking for is going to happen.

The call to spiritual perseverance is not to hang on and do nothing, but to work deliberately, knowing with certainty that God will never be defeated.

_____ **FEBRUARY 22**

The Determination to Save

"The Son of Man did not come to be served, but to serve."
(Matthew 20:28)

If our devotion is to the cause of humanity, we will be quickly defeated and brokenhearted, since we will often be confronted with a great deal of ingratitude.

If we are motivated by our love for God, no amount of ingratitude will be able to hinder us from serving one another.

FEBRUARY 23 _____

The Delight of Sacrifice

*I will very gladly spend and be spent
for your souls.*
(Second Corinthians 12:15)

When someone thinks that to
develop a holy life he must
always be alone with God, he is no
longer of any use to others.

If we are totally surrendered to
Him, we have no goals of our own
to serve.

_____ **FEBRUARY 24**

The Destitution of Service

Though the more abundantly I love you, the less I am loved.
(Second Corinthians 12:15)

The real test of a saint is not one's willingness to preach the gospel, but one's willingness to do something like washing the disciples' feet.

That is, being willing to do those things that seem unimportant in human estimation but count as everything to God.

FEBRUARY 25 _____

Our Misgivings about Jesus

The woman said to Him, "Sir, You have nothing to draw (water) with, and the well is deep." (John 4:11)

My misgivings arise from the fact that I search within to find how He will do what He says. My doubts spring from the depths of my own inferiority.

The Impoverished Ministry of Jesus

Where then do You get that living water? (John 4:11)

The reason some of us are such poor examples of Christianity is that we have failed to recognize that Christ is almighty.

You will know it can be done if you will look to Jesus.

"Do You Now Believe?"

*By this we believe . . . Jesus
answered them, "Do you now
believe?"* (John 16:30–31)

When we do something out of a
sense of duty, it is easy to explain the reasons for our actions to
others.

When we do something out of
obedience to the Lord, there can be
no other explanation—just obedience.

What Do You Want the Lord to Do for You?

"What do you want Me to do for you?" He said, "Lord, that I may receive my sight." (Luke 18:41)

When Jesus asks what we want Him to do for us about the incredible problem that is confronting us, remember that he doesn't work in commonsense ways, but only in supernatural ways.

Once we see Jesus, the impossible things He does in our lives becomes as natural as breathing.

FEBRUARY 29 _____

March

The Piercing Question

"Do you love Me?" (John 21:17)

The true love within our inner spiritual self can be discovered only by experiencing the hurt of this question of Jesus Christ.

This question of the Lord intensifies our sensitivities to the point that this hurt produced by Jesus is the most exquisite pain conceivable.

MARCH 1 _____

Have You Felt the Pain Inflicted by the Lord?

He said to him the third time, . . .
"Do you love Me?" (John 21:17)

Have you ever felt the pain, inflicted by the Lord, at the very center of your being, deep down in the most sensitive area of your life?

The Lord's questions always reveal the true me to myself.

His Commission to Us

"Feed My sheep." (John 21:17)

The goal of the indwelling Holy Spirit is not just to unite us with God, but to do it in such a way that we will be one with the Father in exactly the same way Jesus was. If I love my Lord, I have no business being guided by natural emotions—I have to feed His sheep.

Is This True of Me?

Nor do I count my life dear to myself. (Acts 20:24)

It is easier to serve or work for God without a vision and without a call, because then you are not bothered by what He requires.

Once you receive a commission from Jesus Christ, the memory of what God asks of you will always be there to prod you on to do His will.

Is He Really My Lord?

So that I may finish my race with joy, and the ministry which I received from the Lord Jesus.
(Acts 20:24)

Joy comes from seeing the complete fulfillment of the specific purpose for which I was created and born again, not from successfully doing something of my own choosing.

Jesus is asking for absolute loyalty to His commission, a faithfulness to what we discern when we are in the closest possible fellowship with God.

MARCH 5 _____

Taking the Next Step

In much patience, in tribulations, in needs, in distresses.
(Second Corinthians 6:4)

We lose interest and give up when we have no vision, no encouragement, and no improvement, but only experience our everyday life with its trivial tasks.

Never allow yourself to think that some tasks are beneath your dignity or too insignificant for you to do, and remind yourself of the example of Christ in John 13:1–17.

The Source of Abundant Joy

In all these things we are more than conquerors through Him who loved us. (Romans 8:37)

A saint doesn't know the joy of the Lord in spite of tribulation, but because of it.

The experiences of life, whether they are everyday events or terrifying ones, are powerless to "separate us from the love of God which is in Christ Jesus our Lord" (Romans 8:39).

The Surrendered Life

I have been crucified with Christ.
(Galatians 2:20)

To become one with Jesus Christ, a person must be willing not only to give up sin, but also to surrender his whole way of looking at things.

When people really see themselves as the Lord sees them, . . . what shocks them is the awful nature of the pride of their own hearts opposing Jesus Christ.

Turning Back or Walking with Jesus?

"Do you also want to go away?"
(John 6:67)

When God gives you a clear determination of His will for you, all your striving to maintain that relationship by some particular method is completely unnecessary.

Never try to live your life with God in any other way than His way.

Being an Example of His Message

Preach the word!
(Second Timothy 4:2)

God takes us beyond our own aspirations and ideas for our lives, and molds and shapes us for His purpose, just as He worked in the disciples' lives after Pentecost.

Before God's message can liberate other people, His liberation must first be real in you.

Obedience to the "Heavenly Vision"

I was not disobedient to the heavenly vision. (Acts 26:19)

If we do not apply our beliefs about God to the issues of everyday life, the vision God has given us will never be fulfilled.

We cannot bring the vision to fulfillment through our own efforts, but must live under its inspiration until it fulfills itself.

MARCH 11 _____

Total Surrender

Peter began to say to Him, "See, we have left all and followed You."
(Mark 10:28)

Gaining heaven, being delivered from sin, and being made useful to God are things that should never even be a consideration in real surrender.

Genuine total surrender is a personal sovereign preference for Jesus Christ Himself.

God's Total Surrender to Us

For God so loved the world that He gave . . . (John 3:16)

Salvation means that the Spirit of God has brought me into intimate contact with the true Person of God Himself.

As I am caught up into total surrender to God, I become thrilled with something infinitely greater than myself.

MARCH 13 _____

Yielding

You are that one's slave whom you obey. (Romans 6:16)

Yield for one second to anything in the nature of lust, and although you may hate yourself for having yielded, you become enslaved to that thing.

No release or escape from lust will ever come from any human power, but only through the power of redemption.

The Discipline of Dismay

As they followed they were afraid.
(Mark 10:32)

Jesus Christ had to understand fully every sin and sorrow that human beings could experience, and that is what makes Him seem unfamiliar.

The discipline of dismay is an essential lesson which a disciple must learn.

MARCH 15 _____

The Master Will Judge

*We must all appear before the
judgment seat of Christ.*
(Second Corinthians 5:10)

Live constantly reminding yourself of the judgment seat of
Christ, and walk in the knowledge
of the holiness He has given you.

No power, except the power that
comes from being filled with the
Holy Spirit, can change or prevent
the inherent consequences of sin.

The Servant's Primary Goal

We make it our aim . . . to be well pleasing to Him.
(Second Corinthians 5:9)

It is not a lack of spiritual experience that leads to failure, but a lack of working to keep our eyes focused and on the right goal.

I must learn to relate everything to the primary goal, "to be well pleasing to Him," maintaining it without interruption.

MARCH 17 _____

Will I Bring Myself Up to this Level?

Perfecting holiness in the fear of God. (Second Corinthians 7:1)

God's perspective is that through His promises I will come to recognize His claim of ownership on me.

I must cleanse myself from all filthiness in my flesh and my spirit until both are in harmony with the nature of God.

Abraham's Life of Faith

He went out, not knowing where he was going. (Hebrews 11:8)

Faith is rooted in the knowledge of a Person, and one of the biggest traps we fall into is the belief that if we have faith, God will surely lead us to success in the world.

A life of faith is not a life of one glorious mountain top experience after another, like soaring on eagles' wings, but is a life of day-in and day-out consistency.

MARCH 19 _____

Friendship with God

Shall I hide from Abraham what I am doing? (Genesis 18:17)

When you have a right-standing relationship with God, you have a life of freedom, liberty, and delight.

You are free to make decisions in the light of a perfect and delightful friendship with God, knowing that if your decisions are wrong He will lovingly produce that sense of restraint.

Identified or Simply Interested?

I have been crucified with Christ.
(Galatians 2:20)

I must take my emotional opinions and intellectual beliefs and be willing to turn them into a moral verdict against the nature of sin.

It is no longer a faith in faith, but a faith that transcends all imaginable limits—a faith that only comes from the Son of God.

MARCH 21

The Burning Heart

Did not our heart burn within us?
(Luke 24:32)

If the Spirit of God has stirred you, make as many of your decisions as possible irrevocable, and let the consequences be what they will.

When God gives us a vision, we must transact business with Him at that point, no matter what the cost.

Am I Carnally Minded?

Where there are envy, strife, and divisions among you, are you not carnal? (First Corinthians 3:3)

Never deceive yourself; when carnality is gone you will know it—it is the most real thing you can imagine.

You will never cease to be the most amazed person on earth at what God has done for you on the inside.

MARCH 23 _____

Decreasing for His Purpose

He must increase, but I must decrease. (John 3:30)

John said this was his joy, a stepping aside, an absolute removal of the servant, never to be thought of again.

You may often have to watch Jesus Christ wreck a life before he saves it (see Matthew 10:34).

Maintaining the Proper Relationship

The friend of the bridegroom.
(John 3:29)

If my holiness is not drawing others to Him, it is not the right kind of holiness; it is only an influence which . . . diverts people from heading in the right direction.

A person who is a beautiful saint can be a hindrance in leading people to the Lord by presenting only what Christ has done for him, instead of presenting Jesus Christ Himself.

MARCH 25 _____

Spiritual Vision Through Personal Purity

Blessed are the pure in heart, for they shall see God. (Matthew 5:8)

If the outer level of our spiritual life with God is impaired to the slightest degree, we must put everything aside until we make it right.

A practical help in keeping your personal purity unblemished in your relations with other people is to begin to see them as God does.

Spiritual Vision Through Personal Character

Come up here, and I will show you things which must take place.
(Revelation 4:1)

Your growth in grace is not measured by the fact that you haven't turned back, but that you have an insight and understanding into where you are spiritually.

God has to hide from us what He does, until, due to the growth of our personal character, we get to the level where He is then able to reveal it.

MARCH 27 _____

Isn't There Some Misunderstanding?

"Let us go to Judea again." The disciples said to Him, ". . . are you going there again?" (John 11:7–8)

Many of us are faithful to our ideas about Jesus Christ, but how many of us are faithful to Jesus Himself?

Faith is not intellectual understanding; faith is a deliberate commitment to the Person of Jesus Christ, even when I can't see the way ahead.

_____ **MARCH 28**

Our Lord's Surprise Visits

"You also be ready." (Luke 12:40)

The greatest need is not facing our beliefs or doctrines, or even facing the question of whether or not we are of any use to Him, but the need is to face Him.

Being ready for the Lord's surprise visits will not be brought about by service, but through intense spiritual reality, expecting Jesus Christ at every turn.

MARCH 29

Holiness or Hardness toward God?

He . . . wondered that there was no intercessor. (Isaiah 59:16)

Worship and intercession must go together; one is impossible without the other.

Be a person who worships God and lives in a holy relationship with Him.

Heedfulness or Hypocrisy in Ourselves?

If anyone sees his brother sinning a sin which does not lead to death, he will ask, and He will give him life.
(First John 5:16)

One of the most subtle and illusive burdens God ever places on us as saints is this burden of discernment concerning others.

It is not that we are able to bring God into contact with our minds, but that we awaken ourselves to the point where God is able to convey His mind to us regarding the people for whom we intercede.

MARCH 31 _____

April

Helpful or Heartless toward Others?

It is Christ . . . who also makes intercession for us . . . .the Spirit . . . makes intercession for the saints.
(Romans 8:27, 34)

God continually introduces us to people in whom we have no interest, and unless we are worshiping God the natural tendency is to be heartless toward them.

A heartless Christian must be a terrible grief to our Lord.

The Glory That's Unsurpassed

*The Lord Jesus . . . has sent me that
you may receive your sight.*
(Acts 9:17)

When Paul received his sight he
also received spiritual insight
into the Person of Jesus Christ.

The lasting characteristic of a
spiritual man is the ability to understand correctly the meaning of the
Lord Jesus Christ in his life, and the
ability to explain the purposes of
God to others.

If You Had Known

If you had known . . . ! But now
they are hidden from your eyes.
(Luke 19:42)

More than once God has brought me face to face with a strange god in my life, and I knew that I should have given it up, but I didn't do it.

It is a shocking thing that we can be in the exact place where the Spirit of God should be having His completely unhindered way with us, and yet we only make matters worse.

APRIL 3 _____

The Way to Permanent Faith

Indeed the hour is coming . . . that you will be scattered. (John 16:32)

After we have the perfect relationship with God, through the sanctifying work of the Holy Spirit, our faith must be exercised in the realities of everyday life.

It is certainly not of our own choosing, but God engineers our circumstances to take us there.

His Agony and Our Access

Jesus . . . said to the disciples . . .
"Stay here and watch with Me."
(Matthew 26:36,38)

Gethsemane and Calvary repre-
sent something totally unique—
they are the gateway into life for us.

The agony in Gethsemane was
the agony of the Son of God in ful-
filling His destiny as the Savior of
the world.

The Collision of God and Sin

Who Himself bore our sins in His own body on the tree.
(First Peter 2:24)

There is nothing in time or eternity more absolutely certain and irrefutable than what Jesus Christ accomplished on the Cross—He made it possible for the entire human race to be brought back to a right-standing relationship with God.

The Cross is the gate through which any and every individual can enter into oneness with God.

Why We Lack Understanding

He commanded them that they should tell no one the things they had seen, till the Son of Man had risen from the dead. (Mark 9:9)

We must have a oneness with His risen life before we are prepared to bear any particular truth from Him.

Our own unyielding and headstrong opinions will effectively prevent God from revealing anything to us.

His Resurrection Destiny

Ought not the Christ to have suffered these things and to enter into His glory? (Luke 24:26)

One day we will have a body like His glorious body, but we can know here and now the power and effectiveness of His resurrection and can "walk in newness of life" (Romans 6:4).

The term Holy Spirit is actually another name for the experience of eternal life working in human beings here and now.

_____ **APRIL 8**

Have You Seen Jesus?

*After that, He appeared in another
form to two of them.* (Mark 16:12)

Jesus appears to those for whom
He has done something, but we
cannot order or predict when He
will come.

Jesus must appear to you and to
your friend individually; no one can
see Jesus with your eyes.

APRIL 9 _____

Complete and Effective Decision About Sin

Our old man was crucified with Him, that the body of sin might be done away with, that we should no longer be slaves of sin. (Romans 6:6)

It is the greatest moment in your life once you decide that sin must die in you—not simply be restrained, suppressed, or counteracted, but crucified. Are you prepared to let the Spirit of God search you until you know what the level and nature of sin is in your life?

Complete and Effective Divinity

If we have been united together in the likeness of His death, certainly we also shall be in the likeness of His resurrection. (Romans 6:5)

The proof that I have experienced crucifixion with Jesus is that I have a definite likeness to Him.

The resurrection of Jesus has given Him the authority to give the life of God to me, and the experiences of my life must now be built on the foundation of His life.

APRIL 11 _____

Complete and Effective Dominion

*Death no longer has dominion over
Him. . . . the life that He lives, He
lives to God. Likewise you also,
reckon yourselves to be dead indeed
to sin, but alive to God. . . .*
(Romans 6:9–11)

The life that was in Jesus becomes ours because of His
Cross, once we make the decision to
be identified with Him.

Even the weakest saint can experience the power of the deity of the
Son of God, when he is willing to
"let go."

APRIL 12

What to Do When Your Burden is Overwhelming

Cast your burden on the Lord.
(Psalm 55:22)

God wants us to roll our burdens back on Him—to literally "cast your burden," which He has given you, "on the Lord."

Many servants do not know what to do with their burden, and it produces weariness in their lives.

Inner Invincibility

"Take My yoke upon you and learn from Me." (Matthew 11:29)

The burden that God places on us squeezes the grapes in our lives and produces the wine, but most of us see only the wine and not the burden.

If your life is producing only a whine, instead of the wine, then ruthlessly kick it out.

The Failure to Pay Close Attention

The high places were not removed from Israel. Nevertheless the heart of Asa was loyal all his days.
(Second Chronicles 15:17)

You no more need a day off from spiritual concentration on matters in your life than your heart needs a day off from beating. As you cannot take a day off morally and remain moral, neither can you take a day off spiritually and remain spiritual.

Can You Come Down from the Mountain?

While you have the light, believe in the light. (John 12:36)

Never allow a feeling that was awakened in you on the mountaintop to evaporate.

Never change your decisions, but be sure to make your decisions in the light of what you saw and learned on the mountain.

All or Nothing

When Simon Peter heard that it was the Lord, he put on his outer garment . . . and plunged into the sea. (John 21:7)

The true deep crisis of abandonment, or total surrender, is reached internally, not externally.

Deliberately committing your will to Jesus Christ is a transaction of the will, not of emotion; any positive emotion that results is simply a superficial blessing arising out of the transaction.

Readiness

God called to him . . . And he said,
"Here I am." (Exodus 3:4)

Readiness means having a right relationship to God and having the knowledge of where we are.

Readiness for God means that we are prepared to do the smallest thing or the largest thing—it makes no difference.

Beware of the Least Likely Temptation

Joab had defected to Adonijah, though he had not defected to Absalom. (First Kings 2:28)

You may have just victoriously gone through a great crisis, but now be alert about the things that may appear to be the least likely to tempt you.

Beware of thinking that the areas of your life where you have experienced victory in the past are now the least likely to cause you to stumble and fall.

APRIL 19 _____

Can a Saint Falsely Accuse God?

All the promises of God in Him are Yes, and in Him Amen.
(Second Corinthians 1:20)

We must never measure our spiritual capacity on the basis of our education or intellect; our capacity in spiritual things is measured on the basis of the promises of God. A person who is lazy in the natural realm is always critical, and someone who is lazy in the spiritual realm is critical of God.

Don't Hurt the Lord

"Have I been with you so long, and yet you have not known Me, Philip?" (John 14:9)

The mystery of God is not in what is going to be—it is now, though we look for it to be revealed in the future in some overwhelming, momentous event.

We look for God to exhibit Himself *to* His children, but God only exhibits Himself *in* His children.

The Light that Never Fails

*We all, with unveiled face,
beholding . . . the glory of the Lord.*
(Second Corinthians 3:18)

We must build our faith not on fading lights but on the Light that never fails.

A Christian servant is one who perpetually looks into the face of God and then goes forth to talk to others.

Do You Worship the Work?

We are God's fellow workers.
(First Corinthians 3:9)

We have no right to decide where we should be placed, or to have preconceived ideas as to what God is preparing us to do.

God engineers everything; and wherever he places us, our one supreme goal should be to pour out our lives in wholehearted devotion to Him in that particular work.

APRIL 23 _____

The Warning Against Desiring Spiritual Success

Do not rejoice in this, that the spirits are subject to you. (Luke 10:20)

One life totally devoted to God is of more value to Him than one hundred lives which have been simply awakened by His Spirit.

Unless the worker lives a life that "is hidden with Christ in God" (Colossians 3:3), he is apt to become an irritating dictator to others, instead of an active, living disciple.

"Ready in Season"

Be ready in season and out of season.
(Second Timothy 4:2)

Many of us suffer from the unbalanced tendency to "be ready" only "out of season."

One of the worst traps a Christian worker can fall into is to become obsessed with his own exceptional moments of inspiration.

The Supreme Climb

Take now your son . . . and offer him . . . as a burnt offering on one of the mountains of which I shall tell you. (Genesis 22:2)

If we obey what God says according to our sincere belief, God will break us from those traditional beliefs that misrepresent Him.

If we will stay true to God, God will take us through an ordeal that will serve to bring us into a better knowledge of Himself.

What Do You Want?

Do you seek great things for yourself? (Jeremiah 45:5)

God wants you to be in a much closer relationship with Himself than simply receiving His gifts—He wants you to get to know Him.

If you have only come as far as asking God for things, you have never come to the point of understanding the least bit of what surrender really means.

What You Will Get

*I will give your life to you as a prize
in all places, wherever you go.*
(Jeremiah 45:5)

This is the firm and immovable secret of the Lord to those who trust Him—"I will give your life to you."

The reason people are tired of life is that God has not given them anything—they have not been given their life "as a prize."

Gracious Uncertainty

It has not yet been revealed what we shall be. (First John 3:2)

The nature of the spiritual life is that we are certain in our uncertainty.

We are uncertain of the next step, but we are certain of God.

Spontaneous Love

Love suffers long and is kind.
(First Corinthians 13:4)

The fountains from which love flows are in God, not in us.

When we look back, we will not be able to determine why we did certain things, but we can know that we did them according to the spontaneous nature of His love in us.

May

Faith—Not Emotion

We walk by faith, not by sight.
(Second Corinthians 5:7)

A self-assured saint is of no value to God.

God will give us His touches of inspiration only when He sees that we are not in danger of being led away by them.

The Patience to Wait for the Vision

Though it tarries, wait for it.
(Habakkuk 2:3)

If we have only what we have experienced, we have nothing.

If we have the inspiration of the vision of God, we have more than we can experience.

Vital Intercession

Praying always with all prayer and
supplication in the Spirit.
(Ephesians 6:18)

It is impossible for us to have living and vital intercession unless we are perfectly and completely sure of God.

The greatest destroyer of that confident relationship to God, so necessary for intercession, is our own personal sympathy and preconceived bias.

Vicarious Intercession

Having boldness to enter the Holiest
by the blood of Jesus.
(Hebrews 10:19)

Our ability to approach God is due entirely to the vicarious, or substitutionary, identification of our Lord with sin.

Spiritual stubbornness is the most effective hindrance to intercession, because it is based on a sympathetic "understanding" of things we see in ourselves and others that we think needs no atonement.

Judgment and the Love of God

The time has come for judgment to begin at the house of God.
(First Peter 4:17)

In the teachings of Jesus Christ the element of judgment is always brought out—it is the sign of the love of God.

When the truth is preached, the Spirit of God brings each person face to face with God Himself.

Liberty and the Standards of Jesus

Stand fast therefore in the liberty by which Christ has made us free.
(Galatians 5:1)

Always measure your life solely by the standards of Jesus.

It takes God a long time to get us to stop thinking that unless everyone sees things exactly as we do, they must be wrong.

Building for Eternity

Which of you, intending to build a tower, does not sit down first and count the cost, whether he has enough to finish it. (Luke 14:28)

The conditions of discipleship given to us by our Lord (Luke 14:26, 27, 33) mean that the men and women He is going to use are those in whom He has done everything.

Jesus, as the Master Builder, takes us over so that He may direct and control us completely for His enterprises and His building plans.

The Faith to Persevere

Because you have kept My command to persevere. (Revelation 3:10)

Disaster occurs in your life when you lack the mental composure that comes from establishing yourself on the eternal truth that God is holy love.

If we take the view that eternal life is a life that can face anything, life will become one great romance—a glorious opportunity of seeing wonderful things.

MAY 8 _____

Reaching Beyond Our Grasp

Where there is no revelation, the
people cast off restraint.
(Proverbs 29:18)

People who are totally con-
sumed with idealistic principles
rarely do anything.

If we are eating only out of our
own hand, and doing things solely
on our own initiative without expecting God to come in, we are on a
downward path.

Take the Initiative

Add to your faith virtue.
(Second Peter 1:5)

If you hesitate when God tells you
to do something, you are being
careless, spurning the grace in
which you stand.

If, when a crisis comes, we instinctively turn to God, we will
know that the habit of carefully lis-
tening to God has been formed in
us.

MAY 10 _____

"Love One Another"

Add to your . . . brotherly kindness love. (Second Peter 1:5,7)

The knowledge that God has loved me beyond all limits will compel me to go into the world to love others in the same way.

Neither natural love nor God's divine love will remain and grow in me unless it is nurtured.

The Habit of Having No Habits

*If these things are yours and abound,
you will be neither barren nor
unfruitful.* (Second Peter 1:8)

Our spiritual life continually causes us to focus our attention inwardly for the determined purpose of self-examination.

Love means that there are no visible habits—that your habits are so immersed in the Lord that you practice them without realizing it.

MAY 12 _____

The Habit of Keeping a Clear Conscience

*Strive to have a conscience, without
offense toward God and men.*
(Acts 24:16)

Conscience is the eye of the soul
which looks out either toward
God or toward what we regard as
the highest standard.

The only thing that keeps our
conscience sensitive to Him is the
habit of being open to God on the
inside.

The Habit of Enjoying Adversity

. . . that the life of Jesus also may be manifested in our body.
(Second Corinthians 4:10)

Our circumstances are the means God uses to exhibit just how wonderfully perfect and extraordinarily pure His Son is.

It is one thing to choose adversity, and quite another to enter into adversity through the orchestrating of our circumstances by God's sovereignty.

The Habit of Rising to the Occasion

That you may know what is the hope of His calling. (Ephesians 1:18)

If you are still the same miserable, grouchy person, set on having your own way, then it is a lie to say that God has saved and sanctified you.

The only proper goal of life is that we manifest the Son of God; and when this occurs, all of our dictating of our demands to God disappears.

The Habit of Recognizing God's Provision

You may be partakers of the divine nature. (Second Peter 1:4)

Almighty God will reach to the last grain of sand and the remotest star to bless us if we will only obey Him.

Before God becomes satisfied with us, He will take everything of our so-called wealth, until we learn that He is our Source; "All my springs are in You" (Psalm 87:7).

His Ascension and Our Access

While He blessed them, . . . He was parted from them and carried up into heaven. (Luke 24:51)

Our Lord returned to His original glory, but not simply as the Son of God—He returned to His father as the Son of Man as well.

There is now freedom of access for anyone straight to the very throne of God because of the ascension of the Son of Man.

Living Simply—Yet Focused

Look at the birds of the air . . .
Consider the lilies of the field.
(Matthew 6:26,28)

We cannot discover the source of our natural life through common sense and reasoning, and Jesus is teaching here that growth in our spiritual life comes from concentrating on our Father in heaven. If you want to be of use to God, maintain the proper relationship with Jesus Christ by staying focused on Him.

MAY 18 _____

"Out of the Wreck I Rise"

Who shall separate us from the love of Christ? (Romans 8:35)

It doesn't matter how real or intense the adversities may be; nothing can ever separate the child of God from his relationship to God.

I feel sorry for the Christian who doesn't have something in the circumstances of his life that he wishes was not there.

Taking Possession of Our Own Soul

By your patience possess your souls.
(Luke 21:19)

We fail because we are ignorant of the way God has made us, and we blame things on the devil that are actually the result of our own undisciplined natures.

The problem that most of us are cursed with is simply that we *won't*.

Having God's "Unreasonable" Faith

Seek first the kingdom of God and His righteousness, and all these things shall be added to you.
(Matthew 6:33)

Jesus is saying that the greatest concern of life is to place our relationship with God first and everything else second.

One of the most difficult, yet critical, disciplines of the Christian life is to allow the Holy Spirit to bring us into absolute harmony with this teaching of Jesus.

The Explanation for Our Difficulties

"That they all may be one, as You, Father, are in Me, and I in You; that they also may be one in Us."
(John 17:21)

The things we are going through are either making us sweeter, better, and nobler, or they are making us more critical and fault-finding and more insistent on our own way.

When we understand God's purpose, we will not become small-minded and cynical.

MAY 22

Our Careful Unbelief

*"Do not worry about your life, what
you will eat or what you will drink;
nor about your body, what you will
put on."* (Matthew 6:25)

Jesus summed up common sense
carefulness in the life of a disciple as *unbelief*.

The only cure for unbelief is obedience to the Spirit.

The Delight of Despair

When I saw Him, I fell at His feet as dead. (Revelation 1:17)

There are times when God cannot reveal Himself in any other way than in His majesty, and it is the awesomeness of the vision which brings you to the delight of despair.

Whenever His hand is laid upon you, it gives the sense that "underneath are the everlasting arms" (Deuteronomy 33:27) full of support, provision, comfort and strength.

The Good or the Best?

If you take the left, then I will go to the right; or, if you go to the right, then I will go to the left.
(Genesis 13:9)

As soon as you begin to live the life of faith in God, fascinating and physically gratifying possibilities will open up before you.

God sometimes allows you to get into a place of testing where your own welfare would be the appropriate thing to consider, if you were not living the life of faith.

Thinking of Prayer as Jesus Taught

Pray without ceasing.
(First Thessalonians 5:17)

The correct concept is to think of prayer as the breath in our lungs and the blood from our hearts.

Prayer is not an exercise, it is the life of the saint.

The Life to Know Him

"Tarry in the city of Jerusalem until you are endued with power from on high." (Luke 24:49)

It is not the baptism of the Holy Spirit that changes people, but the power of the ascended Christ coming into their lives through the Holy Spirit.

The baptism of the Holy Spirit does not make you think of time or eternity—it is one amazing glorious now.

Unquestioned Revelation

"In that day you will ask Me nothing." (John 16:23)

In that day when the Lord makes you one with the Father there may be any number of things still hidden to your understanding, but they will not come between your heart and God.

You will come to the place where there is no distance between the Father and you, His child, because the Lord has made you one.

MAY 28 _____

Untroubled Relationship

"In that day you will ask in My name . . . for the Father Himself loves you." (John 16:26–27)

Our Lord does not mean that our lives will be free from external difficulties and uncertainties.

Just as He knew the Father's heart and mind, we too can be lifted by Him into heavenly places through the baptism of the Holy Spirit, so that He can reveal the teachings of God to us.

"Yes—But . . . !

Lord, I will follow You, but . . .
(Luke 9:61)

If a person is ever going to do any-thing worthwhile, there will be times when he must risk everything by his leap in the dark.

By the test of common sense, Jesus Christ's statements may seem mad, but when you test them by the trial of faith, your findings will fill your spirit with the awesome fact that they are the very words of God.

MAY 30 _____

Put God First

Jesus did not commit Himself to them . . . for He knew what was in man. (John 2:24–25)

If I put my trust in human beings first, the end result will be my despair and hopelessness toward everyone.

If I put my trust in human beings, I will become bitter because I have insisted that people be what no person can ever be—absolutely perfect and right.

June

The Staggering Question

He said to me, Son of man, can these bones live? (Ezekiel 37:3)

It is much easier to do something than to trust in God; we see the activity and mistake panic for inspiration.

If the Spirit of God has ever given you a vision of what you are apart from the grace of God, then you know that in reality there is no criminal half as bad as you yourself could be without His grace.

Are You Obsessed by Something?

Who, then, is the man that fears the Lord? (Psalm 25:12)

The abiding awareness of the Christian life is to be God Himself, not just thoughts about Him.

If we are obsessed with God, nothing else can get into our lives—not concerns, nor tribulation, nor worries.

JUNE 2 _____

"The Secret of the Lord"

The secret of the Lord is with those who fear Him. (Psalm 25:14)

What makes God so dear to us is not so much His big blessings to us, but the tiny things, because they show His amazing intimacy with us—He knows every detail of each of our individual lives.

God instructs us in what we choose; that is, He actually guides our common sense.

The Never-Forsaking God

He, Himself has said, "I will never leave you nor forsake you."
(Hebrews 13:5)

"**I** will never leave you"—not for any reason; not my sin, selfishness, stubbornness, nor waywardness.

When there is no major difficulty to overcome, no vision from God, nothing wonderful or beautiful—just the everyday activities of life—do I hear God's assurance even in these?

God's Assurance

He Himself has said . . . So we may boldly say. (Hebrews 13:5–6)

The only way to remove the fear from our lives is to listen to God's assurance to us.

Are we continually filled with enough courage to say, "The Lord is my helper," or are we yielding to fear?

"Work Out" What God "Works In" You

*Work out your own salvation . . . for
it is God who works in you.*
(Philippians 2:12–13)

What causes you to say, "I will not obey" is perversity or stubbornness, and they are never in agreement with God.

The only thing to do with this barrier of stubbornness is to blow it up with "dynamite," and the "dynamite" is obedience to the Holy Spirit.

JUNE 6 _____

The Greatest Source of Power

"Whatever you ask in My name, that I will do." (John 14:13)

True intercession is a hidden ministry that brings forth fruit through which the Father is glorified.

If the central point, or the most powerful influence, of my life is the atonement of the Lord, then every aspect of my life will bear fruit for Him.

What's Next to Do?

*"If you know these things, blessed
are you if you do them."*
(John 13:17)

It is much better to fulfill the purpose of God in your life by discerning His will than it is to perform great acts of self-sacrifice.

Beware of paying attention to or going back to what you once were, when God wants you to be something that you have never been.

Then What's Next to Do?

"Everyone who asks receives."
(Luke 11:10)

"**E**veryone who asks receives" does not mean that you will not *get* if you do not ask, but it means that until you come to the point of asking, you will not *receive* from God.

To be able to receive means that you have to come into the relationship of a child of God, and that you comprehend and appreciate mentally, morally, and with spiritual understanding that these things come from God.

And After That What's Next to Do?

"Seek, and you will find."
(Luke 11:9)

If you ask for things from life instead of from God, "you ask amiss"; that is, you ask out of your desire for self-fulfillment.

It is a humbling experience to knock at God's door—you have to knock with the crucified thief. ". . . to him who knocks it will be opened" (Luke 11:10).

Getting There

"Come to Me." (Matthew 11:28)

The questions that truly matter in life are remarkably few, and they are all answered by these words—"Come to Me."

The attitude necessary for you to come to Him is one where your will has made the determination to let go of everything and deliberately commit it all to Him.

Getting There

They said to Him, "Rabbi . . . where are You staying?" He said to them, "Come and see." (John 1:38–39)

A true disciple is one who has his new name written all over him—self-interest, pride, and self-sufficiency have been completely erased.

Put no condition on your life—let Jesus be everything to you, and He will take you home with Him not only for a day, but for eternity.

Getting There

"Come, follow Me." (Luke 18:22)

The one true mark of a saint of God is the inner creativity that flows from being totally surrendered to Jesus Christ.

A saint realizes that it is God who engineers his circumstances; consequently there are no complaints, only unrestrained surrender to Jesus.

Get Moving!

"Abide in Me." (John 15:4)

"**A**bide in Me"—in intellectual matters, in money matters, in every one of the matters that make human life what it is.

Make the determination to abide in Jesus wherever you are now or wherever you may be placed in the future.

JUNE 14 _____

Get Moving!

Also . . . add to your faith.
(Second Peter 1:5)

Don't always expect God to give you His thrilling moments, but learn to live in those common times of the drudgery of life by the power of God.

I must realize that my obedience even in the smallest detail of life has all of the omnipotent power of the grace of God behind it.

Will You Lay Down Your Life?

"Greater love has no one than this, than to lay down one's life for his friends . . . I have called you friends." (John 15:13,15)

It is much easier to die than to lay down your life day in and day out with the sense of the high calling of God.

We are not made for the bright shining moments of life, but we have to walk in the light of them in our everyday ways.

JUNE 16 _____

Beware of Criticizing Others

"Judge not, that you be not judged."
(Matthew 7:1)

The Holy Spirit is the only one in the proper position to criticize, and He alone is able to show what is wrong without hurting and wounding.

It is impossible to enter into fellowship with God when you are in a critical mood.

Keep Recognizing Jesus

Peter . . . walked on the water to go to Jesus. But when he saw that the wind was boisterous, he was afraid.
(Matthew 14:29-30)

If you are truly recognizing your Lord, you have no business being concerned about how and where He engineers your circumstances.

Let your actual circumstances be what they may, but keep recognizing Jesus, maintaining complete reliance upon Him.

JUNE 18 _____

The Service of Passionate Devotion

"Do you love Me? Tend My sheep."
(John 21:16)

We consider what we do in the way of Christian work as service, yet Jesus Christ calls service to be what we *are* to Him, not what we *do* for Him.

Discipleship is based solely on devotion to Jesus Christ, not on following after a particular belief or doctrine.

Have You Come to "When" Yet?

The Lord restored Job's losses when he prayed for his friends. (Job 42:10)

I must leave myself completely alone in His hands, and then I can begin to pour my life out in the priestly work of intercession.

Whatever circumstances God may place you in, always pray immediately that His atonement may be recognized and as fully understood in the lives of others as it has been in yours.

The Ministry
of the Inner Life

You are . . . a royal priesthood.
(First Peter 2:9)

It is by the right of the atonement by the Cross of Christ that we have become a "royal priesthood."

Don't worry anymore about yourself, but begin to do as Jesus Christ has said, in essence, "Pray for the friend who comes to you at midnight, pray for the saints of God, and pray for all men."

The Unchanged Law of Judgment

With what judgment you judge, you will be judged; and with the measure you use, it will be measured back to you. (Matthew 7:2)

This statement is not some haphazard theory, but it is an eternal law of God.

The greatest characteristic of a saint is humility, as evidenced by being able to say honestly and humbly, "Yes, all those, as well as other evils would have been exhibited in me if it were not for the grace of God."

JUNE 22 _____

"Acquainted with Grief"

*He is . . . a Man of sorrows and
acquainted with grief.* (Isaiah 53:3)

Sin has made the foundation of
our thinking unpredictable, un-
controllable, and irrational.

Sin is the only explanation why
Jesus Christ came to earth, and it is
the explanation of the grief and sorrow of life.

Reconciling Yourself to the Fact of Sin

"This is your hour, and the power of darkness." (Luke 22:53)

You may talk about the lofty virtues of human nature, but there is something in human nature that will mockingly laugh in the face of every principle you have.

Always beware of any assessment of life which does not recognize the fact that there is sin.

Receiving Yourself in the Fires of Sorrow

"What shall I say? 'Father, save Me from this hour'? But for this purpose I came to this hour. 'Father, glorify Your name.'" (John 12:27–28)

Sorrow is one of the biggest facts in life, and there is no use in saying it should not be.

Sin, sorrow, and suffering *are*, and it is not for us to say that God made a mistake in allowing them.

Drawing on the Grace of God—Now

We . . . plead with you not to receive the grace of God in vain.
(Second Corinthians 6:1)

Grace is the overflowing favor of God, and you can always count on it being available to draw upon as needed.

Let circumstances take you where they will, but keep drawing on the grace of God in whatever condition you may find yourself.

JUNE 26 _____

The Overshadowing of God's Personal Deliverance

"I am with you to deliver you," says the Lord. (Jeremiah 1:8)

If our hold on personal property and possessions is not very loose we will have panic, heartache, and distress.

Having the proper outlook is evidence of the deeply rooted belief in the overshadowing of God's personal deliverance.

Held by the Grip of God

I press on, that I may lay hold of that for which Christ Jesus has also laid hold of me. (Philippians 3:12)

There must be unflinching faithfulness to the Word of God, but when you come to personal dealings with others, remember who you are—you are not some special being created in heaven, but a sinner saved by grace.

"One thing I do, . . . I press toward the goal of the prize of the upward call of God in Christ Jesus." (Philippians 3:13–14).

JUNE 28

The Strictest Discipline

"If your right hand causes you to sin, cut it off and cast it from you."
(Matthew 5:30)

When God changes you through regeneration, giving you new life through spiritual re-birth, your life initially has the characteristic of being maimed.

The Christian life is a maimed life initially but Jesus says, "You shall be perfect, just as your Father in heaven is perfect" (Matthew 5:48).

Do It Now!

"Agree with your adversary quickly."
(Matthew 5:25)

From our Lord's standpoint it doesn't matter whether I am cheated or not, but what does matter is that I don't cheat someone else.

The fact that we insist on proving that we are right is almost always a clear indication that we have some point of disobedience.

JUNE 30 _____

July

The Inevitable Penalty

"You will by no means get out of here till you have paid the last penny." (Matthew 5:26)

God is determined to make you pure, holy and right, and He will not allow you to escape from the scrutiny of the Holy Spirit for even one moment.

The moment you are willing for God to change your nature, His re-creating forces will begin to work.

JULY 1 _____

The Conditions of Discipleship

"Whoever of you does not forsake all that he has cannot be My disciple."
(Luke 14:33)

Discipleship means personal, passionate devotion to a Person—our Lord Jesus Christ.

Jesus Christ was always consistent in His relationship to God, and a Christian must be consistent in his relationship to the life of the Son of God in him, not consistent to strict, unyielding doctrines.

The Concentration of Personal Sin

Woe is me, for I am undone!
Because I am a man of unclean lips.
(Isaiah 6:5)

God begins by convicting us of the very thing to which His Spirit has directed our mind's attention.

The experience of our attention being directed to our concentration of personal sin is true in everyone's life, from the greatest of saints to the worst of sinners.

One of God's Great "Don'ts"

Do not fret—it only causes harm.
(Psalm 37:8)

We tend to think that a little anxiety and worry are simply an indication of how wise we really are, yet it is actually a much better indication of just how wicked we are.

Have you been propping up that foolish soul of yours with the idea that your circumstances are too much for God to handle?

Don't Plan Without God

Commit your way to the Lord, trust also in Him, and He shall bring it to pass. (Psalm 37:5)

In spiritual issues it is customary for us to put God first, but we tend to think that it is inappropriate and unnecessary to put Him first in the practical, everyday issues of our lives.

You cannot hoard things for a rainy day if you are truly trusting Christ.

Visions Becoming Reality

The parched ground shall become a pool. (Isaiah 35:7)

God has to take us into the valley and put us through fires and floods to batter us into shape, until He can trust us with the reality of the vision.

The vision that God gives is not some unattainable castle in the sky, but a vision of what God wants you to do down here.

All Efforts of Worth and Excellence Are Difficult

"Enter by the narrow gate . . . because narrow is the gate and difficult is the way which leads to life." (Matthew 7:13–14)

If we fail, it is because we have not yet put into practice what God has placed within us.

If we will obey the Spirit of God and practice in our physical life what God has placed within us by His Spirit, then when a crisis does come we will find that our own nature, as well as the grace of God, will stand by us.

Will to Be Faithful

*Choose for yourself this day whom
you will serve.* (Joshua 24:15)

When God gives me a vision of
truth, there is never a question of what He will do, but only of
what I will do.

Don't consult with other Christians, but simply and freely declare
before Him, "I will serve You."

Will You Examine Yourself?

Joshua said to the people, "You cannot serve the Lord."
(Joshua 24:19)

If we really believe that God meant what He said, just imagine what we would be like!

Do I really dare to let God be to me all that He said He will be?

The Spiritually Lazy Saint

Let us consider one another in order to stir up love and good works, not forsaking the assembling of ourselves together. (Hebrews 10:24–25)

It is a most disturbing thing to be hit squarely in the stomach by someone being used of God to stir us up—someone who is full of spiritual activity.

The real danger in spiritual laziness is that we do not want to be stirred up—all we want to hear about is a spiritual retirement from the world.

The Spiritually Vigorous Saint

. . . that I may know Him.
(Philippians 3:10)

A saint is not to take the initiative toward self-realization, but toward knowing Jesus Christ.

A spiritually vigorous saint never believes that his circumstances simply happen at random, nor does he ever think of his life as being divided into the secular and the sacred.

The Spiritually Self-Seeking Church

Till we all come . . . to the measure of the stature of the fullness of Christ. (Ephesians 4:13)

The church ceases to be spiritual when it becomes self-seeking, only interested in its own organization.

I will suffer great humiliation once I come to acknowledge and understand that I have not really been concerned about Jesus Christ Himself, but only concerned with knowing what He has done for me.

The Price of the Vision

*In the year that King Uzziah died, I
saw the Lord.* (Isaiah 6:1)

Before I can say, "I saw the
Lord," there must be something in my character that conforms
to the likeness of God.

What I need is God's surgical
procedure—His use of external circumstances to bring about internal
purification.

Suffering Afflictions and Going the Second Mile

"I tell you not to resist an evil person. But whoever slaps you on your right cheek, turn the other to him also." (Matthew 5:39)

When you are insulted, you must not only not resent it, but you must make it an opportunity to exhibit the Son of God in your life.

A personal insult becomes an opportunity for a saint to reveal the incredible sweetness of the Lord Jesus.

My Life's Spiritual Honor and Duty

I am a debtor both to Greeks and to barbarians. (Romans 1:14)

Paul sold himself to Jesus Christ and said, in effect, "I am a debtor to everyone on the face of the earth because of the gospel of Jesus; I am free only that I may be an absolute bondservant of His."

Quit praying about yourself and spend your life for the sake of others as the bondservant of Jesus.

The Concept of Divine Control

How much more will your Father who is in heaven give good things to those who ask Him! (Matthew 7:11)

Jesus urges us to keep our minds filled with the concept of God's control over everything, which means that a disciple must maintain an attitude of perfect trust and an eagerness to ask and to seek.

Not even the smallest detail of life happens unless God's will is behind it.

The Miracle of Belief

My speech and my preaching were not with persuasive words of human wisdom. (First Corinthians 2:4)

Real and effective fasting by a preacher is not fasting from food, but fasting from eloquence, from impressive diction, and from everything else that might hinder the gospel of God being presented.

Anything that flatters me in my preaching of the gospel will result in making me a traitor to Jesus.

The Mystery of Believing

He said, "Who are You, Lord?"
(Acts 9:5)

Jesus will never insist that I obey, but if I don't, I have already begun to sign the death certificate of the Son of God in my soul.

It makes no difference to God's grace what an abomination I am, if I will only come to the light.

The Submission of the Believer

"You call Me Teacher and Lord, and you say well, for so I am."
(John 13:13)

Once His life has been created in me through His redemption, I instantly recognize His right to absolute authority over me.

The level of my growth in grace is revealed by the way I look at obedience.

Dependent on God's Presence

Those who wait on the Lord . . .
shall walk and not faint.
(Isaiah 40:31)

Having the reality of God's presence is not dependent on our being in a particular circumstance or place, but is only dependent on our determination to keep the Lord before us continually.

Our problems arise when we refuse to place our trust in the reality of His presence.

The Doorway to the Kingdom

"Blessed are the poor in spirit."
(Matthew 5:3)

I must know Jesus Christ as my Savior before His teaching has any meaning for me other than that of a lofty ideal which only leads to despair.

The knowledge of our own poverty is what brings us to the proper place where Jesus Christ accomplishes His work.

Sanctification

*This is the will of God, your
sanctification.*
(First Thessalonians 4:3)

Sanctification requires our coming to the place of death, but
many of us spend so much time
there that we become morbid.

Sanctification is not something
Jesus puts in me—it is *Himself* in me
(see First Corinthians 1:30).

Sanctification

But of Him you are in Christ Jesus,
who became for us . . .
sanctification.
(First Corinthians 1:30)

It is *His* wonderful life that is imparted to me in sanctification—imparted by faith as a sovereign gift of God's grace.

Sanctification is an impartation, not an imitation.

His Nature and Our Motives

"Unless your righteousness exceeds the righteousness of the scribes and Pharisees, you will by no means enter the kingdom of heaven."
(Matthew 5:20)

The characteristic of a disciple is not that he does good things, but that he is good in his motives, having been made good by the supernatural grace of God.

Jesus Christ does not change human nature—He changes its source, and thereby its motives as well.

Am I Blessed Like This?

"Blessed are . . ." (Matthew 5:3-11)

The teachings of Jesus are all out of proportion when compared to our natural way of looking at things, and they come to us initially with astonishing discomfort.

We gradually have to conform our walk and conversation to the precepts of Jesus Christ as the Holy Spirit applies them to our circumstances.

The Way to Purity

"Those things which proceed out of the mouth come from the heart."
(Matthew 15:18)

Either Jesus Christ is the supreme authority of the human heart, or He is not worth paying any attention to.

When I am open and completely exposed before God, I find that Jesus Christ is right in His diagnosis of me.

The Way to Knowledge

*If anyone wills to do His will, he
shall know concerning the doctrine.*
(John 7:17)

The golden rule to follow to obtain spiritual understanding is not one of intellectual pursuit, but one of obedience.

We disobey and then wonder why we are not growing spiritually.

God's Purpose or Mine?

He made His disciples get into the boat and go before Him to the other side. (Mark 6:45)

If I can stay calm, faithful, and un-confused while in the middle of the turmoil of life, the goal of the purpose of God is being accomplished in me.

God is not working toward a particular finish—His purpose is the process itself.

Do You See Jesus in Your Clouds?

Behold, He is coming with clouds.
(Revelation 1:7)

We have to learn to interpret the mysteries of life in the light of our knowledge of God.

Until we can come face to face with the deepest, darkest fact of life without damaging our view of God's character, we do not yet know Him.

The Teaching of Disillusionment

Jesus did not commit Himself to them . . . for He knew what was in man. (John 2:24–25)

Many of the things in life that inflict the greatest injury, grief, or pain, stem from the fact that we suffer from illusions.

There is only one Being who can completely satisfy to the absolute depth of the hurting human heart and that is the Lord Jesus Christ.

Becoming Entirely His

Let patience have its perfect work,
that you may be perfect and
complete, lacking nothing.
(James 1:4)

We should have no carelessness about us either in the way we worship God, or even in the way we eat and drink.

Beware of becoming careless over the small details of life and saying, "Oh that will have to do for now."

August

Learning About His Ways

*When Jesus finished commanding
His twelve disciples . . . He departed
from there to teach and to preach in
their cities.* (Matthew 11:1)

God wants to instruct us regarding His Son, and He wants to turn our times of prayer into mounts of transfiguration.

When we become certain that God is going to work in a particular way, He will never work in that way again.

The Teaching of Adversity

"In the world you will have tribulation; but be of good cheer, I have overcome the world."
(John 16:33)

God never gives us strength for tomorrow, or for the next hour, but only for the strain of the moment.

A saint can "be of good cheer" even when seemingly defeated by adversities, because victory is absurdly impossible to everyone, except God.

The Compelling Purpose of God

*He . . . said to them, "Behold, we
are going up to Jerusalem."*
(Luke 18:31)

In the natural life our ambitions are our own, but in the Christian life we have no goals of our own.

We are not taken into a conscious agreement with God's purpose—we are taken into God's purpose with no awareness of it at all.

The Brave Friendship of God

He took the twelve aside.
(Luke 18:31)

The only thing of value is being taken into the compelling purpose of God and being made His friends (see First Corinthians 1:26–31).

As Christians we are not here for our own purpose at all—we are here for the purpose of God, and the two are not the same.

The Bewildering Call of God

And all things that are written by the prophets concerning the Son of Man will be accomplished.
(Luke 18:31)

The things that happen do not happen by chance—they happen entirely by the decree of God.

If we have a purpose of our own, it destroys the simplicity and the calm, relaxed pace which should be characteristic of the children of God.

AUGUST 5

The Cross in Prayer

"In that day you will ask in My name." (John 16:26)

The cross represents only one thing for us—complete, entire, absolute identification with the Lord Jesus Christ—and there is nothing in which this identification is more real to us than in prayer.

We are not here to prove that God answers prayer, but to be living trophies of God's grace.

Prayer in the Father's House

"Did you not know that I must be about My Father's business."
(Luke 2:49)

The only abiding reality is God Himself, and His order comes to me moment by moment.

The life of your Lord is to become your vital, simple life, and the way He worked and lived among the people while here on earth must be the way He works and lives in you.

Prayer in the Father's Honor

That Holy One who is to be born will be called the Son of God.
(Luke 1:35)

Is the Son of God praying in me, bringing honor to the Father, or am I dictating my demands to Him?

The more a person knows of the inner life of God's most mature saints, the more he sees what God's purpose really is: to "fill up in my flesh what is lacking in the afflictions of Christ" (Colossians 1:24).

Prayer in the Father's Hearing

Jesus lifted up His eyes and said, "Father, I thank You that You have heard Me." (John 11:41)

Supernatural sense is the gift of His Son, and we should never put our common sense on the throne.

Are we living at such a level of human dependence upon Jesus Christ that His life is being exhibited moment by moment in us?

AUGUST 9

The Holy Suffering of the Saint

Let those who suffer according to the will of God commit their souls to Him in doing good.
(First Peter 4:19)

Choosing to suffer means that there must be something wrong with you, but choosing God's will—even if it means you will suffer—is something very different.

No normal, healthy saint ever chooses suffering; he simply chooses God's will, just as Jesus did, whether it means suffering or not.

This Experience Must Come

Elijah went up by a whirlwind into heaven. And Elisha . . . saw him no more. (Second Kings 2:11–12)

When you come to your wit's end and feel inclined to panic—don't! Stand true to God and He will bring out His truth in a way that will make your life an expression of worship.

The Theology of Resting in God

"Why are you fearful, O you of little faith?" (Matthew 8:26)

What a sharp pain will go through us when we suddenly realize that we could have produced complete and utter joy in the heart of Jesus by remaining absolutely confident in Him, in spite of what we were facing.

It is when a crisis arises that we instantly reveal upon whom we rely.

"Do Not Quench the Spirit"

Do not quench the Spirit.
(First Thessalonians 5:19)

Whenever the Spirit gives you that sense of restraint, call a halt and make things right, or else you will go on quenching and grieving Him without even knowing it.

If you will go on through the crisis, your life will become a hymn of praise to God.

The Discipline of the Lord

*My son, do not despise the
chastening of the Lord, nor be
discouraged when you are rebuked
by Him.* (Hebrews 12:5)

It is very easy to grieve the Spirit
of God; we do it by despising the
discipline of the Lord, or by becoming discouraged when He rebukes
us.

But He has to get me into the
state of mind and spirit where I will
allow Him to sanctify me completely, whatever the cost.

The Evidence of the New Birth

"You must be born again." (John 3:7)

The answer to Nicodemus' question, "How can a man be born when he is old?" is: when he becomes willing to receive into himself a new life that he has never before experienced (John 3:4).

This new life exhibits itself in our conscious repentance and through our unconscious holiness.

AUGUST 15 _____

Does He Know Me?

"He calls His own . . . by name."
(John 10:3)

A person's soul is in grave danger when the knowledge of doctrine surpasses Jesus, avoiding intimate touch with Him.

When His touches will come we never know, but when they do come they are indescribably precious.

Are You Discouraged or Devoted?

Jesus . . . said to him, "You still lack
one thing. Sell all that you have . . .
and come, follow Me." (Luke 18:22)

Jesus says a tremendous amount
to us that we listen to, but do not
actually hear.

Our Lord never pleaded with the
rich young ruler; He never tried to
lure Him—He simply spoke the
strictest words that human ears
have ever heard, and then left him
alone.

Have You Ever Been Speechless with Sorrow?

When he heard this, he became very sorrowful, for he was very rich.
(Luke 18:23)

Rid yourself before God of everything that might be considered a possession until you are a mere conscious human being standing before Him, and then give God that.

Discouragement is disillusioned self-love, and self-love may be love for my devotion to Jesus—not love for Jesus Himself.

Self-Awareness

"Come to Me." (Matthew 11:28)

Self-awareness is the first thing that will upset the completeness of our life in God, and self-awareness continually produces a sense of struggle and turmoil in our lives.

If we will come to Him, asking Him to produce Christ-awareness in us, He will always do it, until we fully learn to abide in Him.

Completeness

"And I will give you rest."
(Matthew 11:28)

Whenever anything begins to disintegrate your life with Jesus Christ, turn to Him at once, asking Him to re-establish your rest.

Simply ask the Lord to give you Christ-awareness, and He will steady you until your completeness in Him is absolute.

The Ministry of the Unnoticed

"Blessed are the poor in spirit."
(Matthew 5:3)

At the foundation of Jesus Christ's kingdom is the genuine loveliness of those who are commonplace.

I cannot enter His kingdom by virtue of my goodness—I can only enter it as an absolute pauper.

"I Indeed . . . But He"

*I indeed baptize you with water . . .
but He . . . will baptize you with the
Holy Spirit and fire.* (Matthew 3:11)

Repentance does not cause a sense of sin—it causes a sense of inexpressible unworthiness.

The only experience that those who are baptized with the Holy Spirit are ever conscious of is the experience of sensing their absolute unworthiness.

Prayer—Battle in "The Secret Place"

*When you pray, go into your room,
and when you have shut your door,
pray to your Father who is in the
secret place; and your Father who
sees in secret will reward you openly.*
(Matthew 6:6)

The great battle in private prayer is overcoming this problem of our idle and wandering thinking.

Enter into "the secret place," and you will find that God was right in the middle of your everyday circumstances all the time.

AUGUST 23 _____

The Spiritual Search

"What man is there among you who, if his son asks for bread, will give him a stone?" (Matthew 7:9)

We mistake defiance for devotion, arguing with God instead of surrendering.

There is no use praying unless we are living as children of God.

Sacrifice and Friendship

"I have called you friends."
(John 15:15)

Wrapping — We will never know the joy of self-sacrifice until we surrender in every detail of our lives.

As soon as we totally surrender, abandoning ourselves to Jesus, the Holy Spirit gives us a taste of His joy.

Are You Ever Troubled?

"Peace I leave with you, My peace I give to you. . ."(John 14:27)

Allowing anything to hide the face of Jesus Christ from you either causes you to become troubled or gives you a false sense of security.

With regard to the problem that is pressing in on you right now, are you "looking unto Jesus" (Hebrews 12:2) and receiving peace from Him?

Living Your Theology

"Walk while you have the light, lest darkness overtake you." (John 12:35)

Beware of any belief that makes you self-indulgent or self-gratifying; that belief came from the pit of hell itself, regardless of how beautiful it may sound.

Every detail of your life, whether physical, moral, or spiritual, is to be judged and measured by the standard of the atonement by the Cross of Christ.

The Purpose of Prayer

One of His disciples said to Him,
"Lord, teach us to pray." (Luke 11:1)

We look upon prayer simply as a means of getting things for ourselves, but the biblical purpose of prayer is that we may get to know God Himself.

To say that "prayer changes things" is not as close to the truth as saying, "Prayer changes me and then I change things."

The Unsurpassed Intimacy of Tested Faith

Jesus said to her, "Did I not say to you that if you would believe you would see the glory of God?"
(John 11:40)

Every time my theology becomes clear to my own mind, I encounter something that contradicts it.

Faith must be tested, because it can only become your intimate possession through conflict.

Usefulness or Relationship?

"Do not rejoice in this, that the spirits are subject to you, but rather rejoice because your names are written in heaven." (Luke 10:20)

Once you have the right relationship with God through salvation and sanctification, remember that whatever your circumstances may be, you have been placed in them by God.

God uses the reaction of your life to your circumstances to fulfill His purpose, as long as you continue to "walk in the light as He is in the light" (First John 1:7).

AUGUST 30

"My Joy . . . Your Joy"

*"These things I have spoken to you,
that My joy may remain in you, and
that your joy may be full."*
(John 15:11)

The first thing that will hinder this joy is the subtle irritability caused by giving too much thought to our circumstances.

The lives that have been the greatest blessing to you are the lives of those people who themselves were unaware of having been a blessing.

September

Destined to Be Holy

It is written, "Be holy, for I am holy." (First Peter 1:16)

God is not some eternal blessing machine for people to use, and He did not come to save us out of pity—He came to save us because He created us to be holy.

Holiness is not simply what God gives me, but what God has given me that is being exhibited in my life.

SEPTEMBER 1 _____

A Life of Pure and Holy Sacrifice

"He who believes in Me . . . out of his heart will flow . . ." (John 7:38)

His purpose is not the development of a person—His purpose is to make a person exactly like Himself, and the Son of God is characterized by self-expenditure.

Our Lord is filled with overflowing joy whenever He sees any of us not being bound by a particular set of rules, but being totally surrendered to Him.

Pouring Out the Water of Satisfaction

He would not drink it, but poured it out to the Lord.
(Second Samuel 23:16)

You must sacrifice a blessing, pouring it out to God—something that your common sense says is an absurd waste.

As soon as I realize that something is too wonderful for me, that I am not worthy to receive it, and that it is not meant for a human being at all, I must pour it out "to the Lord."

SEPTEMBER 3 _____

His!

"They were Yours, You gave them to Me." (John 17:6)

The Holy Spirit interprets and explains the nature of Jesus to me to make me one with my Lord, not that I might simply become a trophy for His showcase.

I may prefer to belong to my mother, or to my wife, or to myself, but if that is the case, then, Jesus said "[You] cannot be My disciple."

_____ **SEPTEMBER 4**

Watching with Jesus

"Stay here and watch with Me."
(Matthew 26:38)

"**W**atch with Me," Jesus was saying, in effect, "Watch with no private point of view at all, but watch solely and entirely with Me."

"You shall receive power when the Holy Spirit has come upon you" (Acts 1:8), meant that the disciples learned to watch with Him the rest of their lives.

SEPTEMBER 5 _____

The Far-Reaching Rivers of Life

"He who believes in Me . . . out of his heart will flow rivers of living water." (John 7:38)

Never allow anything to come between you and Jesus Christ—not emotion nor experience—nothing must keep you from the one great sovereign Source.

God has been opening up wonderful truths to our minds, and every point He has opened up is another indication of the wider power of the river that He will flow through us.

Fountains of Blessings

"The water that I shall give him will become in him a fountain of water springing up into everlasting life."
(John 4:14)

If you find that His life is not springing up as it should, you are to blame—something is obstructing the flow.

We are to be fountains through which Jesus can flow as "rivers of living water" in blessing to everyone.

SEPTEMBER 7 _____

Do It Yourself

*Casting down arguments and every
high thing that exalts itself against
the knowledge of God.*
(Second Corinthians 10:5)

Every theory or thought that
raises itself up as a fortified barrier "against the knowledge of God"
is to be determinedly demolished
by drawing on God's power.

The warfare is not against sin; we
can never fight against sin—Jesus
Christ conquered that in His redemption of us.

_____ **SEPTEMBER 8**

Do It Yourself

*Bringing every thought into captivity
to the obedience of Christ.*
(Second Corinthians 10:5)

So much Christian work today
has never been disciplined, but
has simply come into being by im-
pulse!

True determination and zeal are
found in obeying God, not in the inclination to serve Him that arises
from our own undisciplined human
nature.

SEPTEMBER 9 _____

Missionary Weapons

"When you were under the fig tree, I saw you." (John 1:48)

If you are not doing the task that is closest to you now, which God has engineered into your life, when the crisis comes, instead of being fit for battle, you will be revealed as being unfit.

A private relationship of worshiping God is the greatest essential element of spiritual fitness.

_____ **SEPTEMBER 10**

Missionary Weapons

*"If I then, your Lord and Teacher,
have washed your feet, you also
ought to wash one another's feet."*
(John 13:14)

The very character we exhibit in
our present surroundings is an
indication of what we will be like in
other surroundings.

It takes God Almighty Incarnate
in us to do the most menial duty as
it ought to be done.

Going Through Spiritual Confusion

Jesus answered and said, "You do not know what you ask."
(Matthew 20:22)

If all you see is a shadow on the face of the Father right now, hang on to the fact that He will ultimately give you clear understanding and will justify Himself in everything that He has allowed to come into your life.

Stand firm in faith, believing that what Jesus said is true, although you do not understand what God is doing.

_____ **SEPTEMBER 12**

After Surrender—Then What?

"I have finished the work which You have given Me to do." (John 17:4)

The surrender is not simply surrender of our external life but surrender of our will—and once that is done, surrender is complete.

Your entire life should be characterized by an eagerness to maintain unbroken fellowship and oneness with God.

SEPTEMBER 13 _____

Arguments or Obedience?

The simplicity that is in Christ.
(Second Corinthians 11:3)

You cannot think through spiritual confusion to make things clear; to make things clear, you must obey.

Even the very smallest thing that we allow in our lives that is not under the control of the Holy Spirit is completely sufficient to account for spiritual confusion.

SEPTEMBER 14

What to Renounce

We have renounced the hidden
things of shame.
(Second Corinthians 4:2)

You must maintain continual watchfulness so that nothing arises in your life that would cause you shame.

Never dull your sense of being your utmost for His highest—your best for His glory.

Praying to God in Secret

"When you pray, go into your room, and when you have shut your door, pray to your Father who is in the secret place." (Matthew 6:6)

Prayer is coming into perfect fellowship and oneness with God. Find an inner room in which to pray where no one even knows you are praying, shut the door, and talk to God in secret.

Is There Good in Temptation?

*No temptation has overtaken you
except such as is common to man.*
(First Corinthians 10:13)

A person's inner nature, what he possesses in the inner, spiritual part of his being, determines what he is tempted by on the outside.

Beware of thinking that you are tempted as no one else—what you go through is the common inheritance of the human race, not something that no one has ever before endured.

SEPTEMBER 17 _____

His Temptation and Ours

*We do not have a High Priest who
cannot sympathize with our
weaknesses, but was in all points
tempted as we are, yet without sin.*
(Hebrews 4:15)

Satan does not come to us on the premise of tempting us to sin, but on the premise of shifting our point of view, and only the Spirit of God can detect this as temptation.

Jesus went through the temptation "without sin," and He retained all the possessions of His spiritual nature completely intact.

Are You Going On with Jesus?

"You are those who have continued with Me in My trials." (Luke 22:28)

Watch when God changes your circumstances to see whether you are going on with Jesus, or siding with the world, the flesh, and the devil.

It is God who engineers our circumstances, and whatever they may be we must see that we face them while continually abiding with Him in His temptations.

SEPTEMBER 19 _____

The Divine Commandment of Life

"Be perfect, just as your Father in heaven is perfect." (Matthew 5:48)

God's life in us expresses itself as God's life, not as human life trying to be godly.

When we come in contact with things that create confusion and a flurry of activity, we find to our own amazement that we have the power to stay wonderfully poised even in the center of it all.

The Missionary's Predestined Purpose

Now the Lord says, who formed Me from the womb to be His Servant.
(Isaiah 49:5)

The first thing that happens after we recognize our election by God in Christ Jesus is the destruction of our preconceived ideas and our narrow-minded thinking.

We must continually keep our soul open to the fact of God's creative purpose, and never confuse or cloud it with our own intentions.

SEPTEMBER 21

The Missionary's Master and Teacher

"You call Me Teacher and Lord, and you say well, for so I am . . . I say to you, a servant is not greater than his master." (John 13:13,16)

Having a master and teacher means that there is someone who knows me better than I know myself, who understands the remotest depths of my heart and is able to satisfy them.

It means having someone who has made me secure in the knowledge that he has met and solved all the doubts, uncertainties, and problems in my mind.

SEPTEMBER 22

The Missionary's Goal

He . . . said to them, "Behold, we
are going up to Jerusalem."
(Luke 18:31)

In our natural life our ambitions change, but in the Christian life the goal is given at the very beginning, and the beginning and the end are exactly the same, namely our Lord Himself.

The goal of the missionary is to do God's will, not to be useful or to win the lost.

The "Go" of Preparation

"First be reconciled to your brother, and then come and offer your gift."
(Matthew 5:24)

The Christian life requires preparation and more preparation.

If it is important enough for the Spirit of God to bring it to your mind, it is the very thing He is detecting in you.

The "Go" of Relationship

"Whoever compels you to go one mile, go with him two."
(Matthew 5:41)

J esus Christ demands that His disciple does not allow even the slightest trace of resentment in his heart when faced with tyranny and injustice.

The Sermon on the Mount is not some unattainable goal; it is a statement of what will happen in me when Jesus Christ has changed my nature by putting His nature in me.

SEPTEMBER 25

The "Go" of Reconciliation

"If you . . . remember that your brother has something against you."
(Matthew 5:23)

Never object to the intense sensitivity of the Spirit of God in you when He is instructing you down to the smallest detail.

The true mark of the saint is that he can waive his own rights and obey the Lord Jesus.

The "Go" of Renunciation

Someone said to Him, "Lord, I will follow You wherever You go."
(Luke 9:57)

If the Spirit of God brings to your mind a word of the Lord that hurts you, you can be sure that there is something in you that He wants to hurt to the point of its death.

Once the call of God comes to you, start going and never stop.

SEPTEMBER 27 _____

The "Go" of Unconditional Identification

"Go your way, sell whatever you have and give to the poor . . . and come, take up the cross, and follow Me." (Mark 10:21)

Jesus' primary consideration is my absolute annihilation of my right to myself and my identification with Him.

Very few of us truly know what is meant by the absolute "go" of unconditional identification with, and abandonment and surrender to, Jesus.

SEPTEMBER 28

The Awareness of the Call

Yes, woe to me if I do not preach the gospel. (First Corinthians 9:16)

The realization of the call in a person's life may come like a clap of thunder or it may dawn gradually.

At any moment the sudden awareness of this incalculable, supernatural, surprising call that has taken hold of your life may break through—"I chose you" (John 15:16).

The Assigning of the Call

I now rejoice in my sufferings for you, and fill up in my flesh what is lacking in the afflictions of Christ, for the sake of His body, which is the church. (Colossians 1:24)

God can never make us into wine if we object to the fingers He chooses to use to crush us.

If we are ever going to be made into wine, we will have to be crushed—you cannot drink grapes.

October

The Place of Exaltation

*Jesus took . . . them up on a high
mountain apart by themselves.*
(Mark 9:2)

The mountaintop is not meant to
teach us anything, it is meant to
make us something.

We are made for the valley and
the ordinary things of life, and that
is where we have to prove our stam-
ina and strength.

The Place of Humiliation

If You can do anything, have compassion on us and help us.
(Mark 9:22)

After every time of exaltation, we are brought down with a sudden rush into things as they really are, where it is neither beautiful, poetic, nor thrilling.

God wants us to be at the drab everyday level, where we live in the valley according to our personal relationship with Him.

OCTOBER 2 _____

The Place of Ministry

He said to them, "This kind [of unclean spirit] can come out by nothing but prayer and fasting."
(Mark 9:29)

When you are brought face to face with a difficult situation and nothing happens externally, you can still know that freedom and release will be given because of your continued concentration on Jesus Christ.

Your duty in service and ministry is to see that there is nothing between Jesus and yourself.

The Vision and the Reality

. . . to those who are . . . called to be saints. (First Corinthians 1:2)

We are not quite prepared for the bumps and bruises that must come if we are going to be turned into the shape of the vision.

Isn't it piercing to realize that God not only knows where we live, but also knows the gutters into which we crawl.

The Nature of Degeneration

*Just as through one man sin entered
the world, and death through sin,
and thus death spread to all men,
because all sinned. . .*
(Romans 5:12)

Sin is something I am born with
and cannot touch—only God
touches sin through redemption.

Condemnation comes when I realize that Jesus Christ came to deliver me from this heredity of sin,
and yet I refuse to let Him do so.

The Nature of Regeneration

When it pleased God . . . to reveal His Son in me. . .
(Galatians 1:15–16)

If Jesus Christ is truly a regenerator, someone who can put His own heredity of holiness in me, then I can begin to see what He means when He says that I have to be holy.

Redemption means that I can be delivered from the heredity of sin, and that through Jesus Christ I can receive a pure and spotless heredity, namely, the Holy Spirit.

OCTOBER 6 _____

The Nature of Reconciliation

He made Him who knew no sin to be sin for us, that we might become the righteousness of God in Him.
(Second Corinthians 5:21)

The revealed truth of the Bible is not that Jesus Christ took on Himself our fleshly sins, but that He took on Himself the heredity of sin that no man can ever touch.

God made His own Son "to be sin" that He might make the sinner into a saint.

Coming to Jesus

"Come to Me." (Matthew 11:28)

As long as you have even the least bit of spiritual disrespect, it will always reveal itself in the fact that you are expecting God to tell you to do something very big, and yet all He is telling you to do is to "Come . . ."

Just think of the invincible, unconquerable, and untiring patience of Jesus, who lovingly says, "Come to Me."

OCTOBER 8

Building on an Atonement

Present . . . your members as instruments of righteousness to God.
(Romans 6:13)

Every time I obey, the absolute deity of God is on my side, so that the grace of God and my natural obedience are in perfect agreement.

Obedience means that I have completely placed my trust in the atonement, and my obedience is immediately met by the delight of the supernatural grace of God.

How Will I Know?

Jesus answered and said, "I thank You Father . . . that You have hidden these things from the wise and prudent and have revealed them to babes." (Matthew 11:25)

Let God's truth work into you by immersing yourself in it, not by worrying into it.

You could read volumes on the work of the Holy Spirit, when five minutes of total, uncompromising obedience would make things as clear as sunlight.

OCTOBER 10 _____

God's Silence—Then What?

When He heard that he was sick, He stayed two more days in the place where He was. (John 11:6)

If God has given you a silence, then praise Him—He is bringing you into the mainstream of His purposes.

A wonderful thing about God's silence is that His stillness is contagious—it gets into you, causing you to become perfectly confident so that you can honestly say, "I know that God has heard me."

Getting into God's Stride

Enoch walked with God.
(Genesis 5:24)

It is painful work to get in step with God and to keep pace with Him—it means getting your second wind spiritually.

Spiritual truth is learned through the atmosphere that surrounds us, not through intellectual reasoning.

Individual Discouragement and Personal Growth

When Moses was grown . . . he went out to his brethren and looked at their burdens. (Exodus 2:11)

We may have the vision of God and a very clear understanding of what God wants, and yet when we start to do it, there comes something equivalent to Moses' forty years in the wilderness.

If you are going through a time of discouragement, there is a time of great personal growth ahead.

The Key to the Missionary's Work

Jesus came and spoke to them, saying, "All authority has been given to Me in heaven and on earth. Go therefore and make disciples of all nations." (Matthew 28:18–19)

If I want to know the universal sovereignty of Christ, I must know Him myself.

Where we are placed is then a matter of indifference to us, because God sovereignly engineers our *goings*.

OCTOBER 14 _____

The Key to the Missionary's Message

*He Himself is the propitiation for
our sins, and not for ours only but
also for the whole world.*
(First John 2:2)

The greatest message of limitless
importance is that "He Himself
is the propitiation for our sins. . .

When the Holy Spirit comes into
me, He simply brings me into oneness with the Lord Jesus.

The Key to the Master's Orders

"Pray the Lord of the harvest to send out laborers into His harvest."
(Matthew 9:38)

In the natural realm, prayer is not practical, but absurd.

We stay busy at work, while people all around us are ripe and ready to be harvested; we do not reap even one of them, but simply waste our Lord's time in over-energized activities and programs.

OCTOBER 16 _____

The Key to the Greater Work

"He who believes in Me, . . . greater works than these he will do, because I go to My Father." (John 14:12)

Wherever God has placed you and whatever your circumstances, you should pray, continually offering up prayers to Him.

When you labor at prayer, from God's perspective there are always results.

The Key to the Missionary's Devotion

They went forth for His name's sake.
(Third John 7)

Faithfulness to Jesus Christ is the supernatural work of redemption that has been performed in me by the Holy Spirit.

The men and women our Lord sends out on His endeavors are ordinary human people, but people who are controlled by their devotion to Him.

OCTOBER 18 _____

The Unheeded Secret

Jesus answered, "My kingdom is not of this world." (John 18:36)

The great enemy of the Lord Jesus Christ today is the ideal of practical work that has no basis in the New Testament but comes from the systems of the world.

You have no idea of where or how God is going to engineer your future circumstances.

Is God's Will My Will?

This is the will of God, your sanctification.
(First Thessalonians 4:3)

Sanctification is not a question of whether God is willing to sanctify me—is it *my* will?

Sanctification makes me one with Jesus Christ, and in Him with God, and it is accomplished only through the magnificent atonement of Christ.

OCTOBER 20 _____

Impulsiveness or Discipleship

But you, beloved, building yourselves up on your most holy faith . . . (Jude 20)

It does require the supernatural grace of God to live twenty-four hours of every day as a saint, . . . living an ordinary, unnoticed and ignored existence . . .

We have to be exceptional in the ordinary things of life, and holy on the ordinary streets, among ordinary people—and this is not learned in five minutes.

The Witness of the Spirit

The Spirit Himself bears witness with our spirit. (Romans 8:16)

We want the witness of the Spirit before we have done what God tells us to do.

We are inclined to mistake the simplicity that comes from our natural common sense decisions for the witness of the Spirit, but the Spirit witnesses only to His own nature, and to the work of redemption, never to our reason.

Nothing of the Old Life!

If anyone is in Christ, he is a new creation; old things have passed away; behold, all things have become new.
(Second Corinthians 5:17)

Our Lord never tolerates our prejudices—He is directly opposed to them and puts them to death.

Once we truly see God at work, we will never be concerned again about the things that happen, because we are actually trusting in our Father in heaven.

The Proper Perspective

Thanks be to God who always leads us in triumph in Christ.
(Second Corinthians 2:14)

Be careful that you vigorously maintain God's perspective, and remember that it must be done every day, little by little.

We are not on display in God's showcase—we are here to exhibit only one thing—the "captivity [of our lives] to the obedience of Christ."

Submitting to God's Purpose

*I have become all things to all men,
that I might by all means save some.*
(First Corinthians 9:22)

Unless we have the right purpose intellectually in our minds and lovingly in our hearts, we will very quickly be diverted from being useful to God.

God is at work bending, breaking, molding, and doing exactly as He chooses.

_____ **OCTOBER 25**

What Is a Missionary?

Jesus said to them again, "As the Father has sent Me, I also send you."
· (John 20:21)

Personal attachment to the Lord Jesus and to His perspective is the one thing that must not be overlooked.

In missionary work the great danger is that God's call will be replaced by the needs of the people.

OCTOBER 26 _____

The Method of Missions

"Go therefore and make disciples of all the nations." (Matthew 28:19)

Remember that there is a passion for souls that does not come from God, but from our desire to make converts to our point of view.

Am I wise enough in God's sight, but foolish enough according to the wisdom of the world, to trust in what Jesus Christ has said?

Justification by Faith

If when we were enemies we were reconciled to God through the death of His Son, much more, having been reconciled, we shall be saved by His life. (Romans 5:10)

It is not repentance that saves me—repentance is only the sign that I realize what God has done through Christ Jesus.

The supernatural becomes natural to us through the miracle of God and there is the realization of what Jesus Christ has already done.

OCTOBER 28 _____

Substitution

He made Him who knew no sin to be sin for us, that we might become the righteousness of God in Him.
(Second Corinthians 5:21)

We are acceptable to God not because we have obeyed, nor because we have promised to give up things, but because of the death of Christ, and for no other reason.

We say that Jesus Christ came to reveal the loving kindness of God, but the New Testament says that He came to take "away the sins of the world!" (John 1:29).

Faith

Without faith it is impossible to please Him. (Hebrews 11:6)

Faith always works in a personal way, because the purpose of God is to see that perfect faith is made real in His children.

God brings us into particular circumstances to educate our faith, because the nature of faith is to make the object of our faith very real to us.

The Trial of Faith

"If you have faith as a mustard seed . . . nothing will be impossible for you." (Matthew 17:20)

God wants you to understand that it is a life of *faith*, not a life of emotional enjoyment of His blessings.

The real trial of faith is not that we find it difficult to trust God, but that God's character must be proven as trustworthy in our own minds.

November

You Are Not Your Own

*Do you not know that . . . you are
not your own?*
(First Corinthians 6:19)

There is no such thing as a private life for a man or woman who is intimately aware of and shares in the sufferings of Jesus Christ.

God divides the private life of His saints and makes it a highway for the world on one hand and for Himself on the other.

Obedience or
Independence?

"If you love Me, keep my commandments." (John 14:15)

Our Lord stresses very definitely what we ought to do, but He never forces us to do it.

If my relationship to Him is that of love, I will do what He says without hesitation.

A Bondservant of Jesus

I have been crucified with Christ; it is no longer I who live, but Christ lives in me. (Galatians 2:20)

These words mean the breaking and collapse of my independence brought about by my own hands, and the surrendering of my life to the supremacy of the Lord Jesus.

Will we allow Him to help Himself to us, or are we more concerned with our own ideas of what we are going to be?

The Authority of Truth

Draw near to God and He will draw near to you. (James 4:8)

Refusing to act leaves a person paralyzed, ... But once he acts, he is never the same.

The dominating power of the world, the flesh, and the devil is now paralyzed; because your act has joined you to God and tapped you in to His redemptive power.

Partakers of His Sufferings

. . . But rejoice to the extent that you partake of Christ's sufferings. . .
(First Peter 4:13)

God will take you through a number of experiences designed to make you useful in His hands, and to enable you to understand what takes place in the lives of others.

. . . Suddenly we come to a place of enlightenment, and realize—"God has strengthened me and I didn't even know it!"

Intimate Theology

"Do you believe this?" (John 11:26)

Your theology is about to become a very personal belief when a personal problem brings the awareness of our personal need.

I am staggered when I think how foolish I have been in not trusting Him earlier.

The Undetected Sacredness of Circumstances

We know that all things work together for good to those who love God. (Romans 8:28)

The circumstances of a saint's life are ordained of God.

God by His providence brings you into circumstances that you can't understand at all, but the Spirit of God understands.

The Unrivaled Power of Prayer

We do not know what we should pray for as we ought, but the Spirit Himself makes intercession for us with groanings which cannot be uttered. (Romans 8:26)

We don't often realize that the Holy Spirit Himself prays prayers in us which we cannot utter ourselves.

We have to remember that our conscious life, even though only a small part of our total person, is to be regarded by us as a "temple of the Holy Spirit."

NOVEMBER 8 _____

Sacred Service

I now rejoice in my sufferings for you, and fill up in my flesh what is lacking in the afflictions of Christ.
(Colossians 1:24)

When we preach the historical facts of the life and death of our Lord as they are conveyed in the New Testament, our words are made sacred.

We must make sure that we are living in such harmony with God that as we proclaim His truth He can create in others those things which He alone can do.

Fellowship in the Gospel

Fellow laborer in the gospel of Christ. (First Thessalonians 3:2)

If you seek great things for yourself, thinking, "God has called me for this and for that," you barricade God from using you.

I must learn that the purpose of my life belongs to God, not me.

The Supreme Climb

He said, "Take now your son."
(Genesis 22:2)

If God has made your cup sweet, drink it with grace; or even if He has made it bitter, drink it in communion with Him.

You must go through the trial before you have any right to pronounce a verdict, because by going through the trial you learn to know God better.

The Changed Life

If anyone is in Christ, he is a new creation; old things have passed away; behold, all things have become new.
(Second Corinthians 5:17)

The work of salvation means that in your real life things are dramatically changed.

If you still yearn for the old things, it is absurd to talk about being born from above—you are deceiving yourself.

Faith or Experience?

The Son of God, who loved me and
gave Himself for me.
(Galatians 2:20)

Think who the New Testament says Jesus Christ is, and then think of the despicable meagerness of the miserable faith we exhibit.

Our lives should be an absolute hymn of praise resulting from perfect, irrepressible, triumphant belief.

Discovering Divine Design

As for me, being on the way, the Lord led me. (Genesis 24:27)

We should be so one with God that we don't need to ask continually for guidance.

If we are born of God we will see His guiding hand and give Him the credit.

"What Is That to You?"

Peter . . . said to Jesus, "But Lord, what about this man?" Jesus said to him, ". . . what is that to you? You follow Me." (John 21:21–22)

Maturity is produced in the life of a child of God on the unconscious level, until we become so totally surrendered to God that we are not even aware of being used by Him.

A saint is never consciously a saint—a saint is consciously dependent on God.

NOVEMBER 15

Still Human!

. . . whatever you do, do all to the glory of God.
(First Corinthians 10:31)

We have a tendency to look for wonder in our experience, and we mistake heroic actions for real heroes.

We tend to set up success in Christian work as our purpose, but our purpose should be to display the glory of God in human life in our everyday human conditions.

NOVEMBER 16 _____

The Eternal Goal

"By Myself I have sworn," says the Lord, "Because you have done this thing . . . I will bless you."
(Genesis 22:16–17)

This work of obedience is the evidence that the nature of God is in me.

The promises of God are of no value to us until, through obedience, we come to understand the nature of God.

Winning into Freedom

"If the Son makes you free, you shall be free indeed." (John 8:36)

We are designed with a great capacity for God, but sin, our own individuality, and wrong thinking keep us from getting to Him.

We tend to rely on our own energy, instead of being energized by the power that comes from identification with Jesus.

"When He Has Come"

"When He has come, he will convict the world of sin." (John 16:8)

The only basis for which God can forgive me is the Cross of Christ.

Forgiveness means that I am forgiven into a newly created relationship which identifies me with God in Christ.

The Forgiveness of God

*In Him we have . . . the forgiveness
of sins.* (Ephesians 1:7)

Forgiveness is the divine miracle
of grace.

The thing that awakens the deepest fountain of gratitude in a human
being is that God has forgiven his
sin.

"It is Finished!"

"I have finished the work which You have given Me to do." (John 17:4)

The greatest note of triumph ever sounded in the ears of a startled universe was that sounded on the Cross of Christ—"It is finished!" (John 19:30)

That is the final word in the Redemption of humankind.

Shallow and Profound

*Whether you eat or drink, or
whatever you do, do all to the glory
of God.* (First Corinthians 10:31)

Beware of allowing yourself to
think that the shallow aspects
of life are not ordained by God; they
are ordained by Him equally as
much as the profound.

Even the shallow things of life,
such as eating and drinking, walk-
ing and talking, are ordained by
God.

NOVEMBER 22 _____

The Distraction of Contempt

Have mercy on us, O Lord, have mercy on us! For we are exceedingly filled with contempt. (Psalm 123:3)

Our state of mind can be the enemy that penetrates right into our soul and distracts our mind from God.

Until we get back into a quiet mood before Him, our faith is of no value, and our confidence in the flesh and in human ingenuity is what rules our lives.

Direction of Focus

*Behold, as the eyes of servants look
to the hand of their masters . . . , so
our eyes look to the Lord our God.*
(Psalm 123:2)

Just as the eyes of a servant
are riveted on his master, our
eyes should be directed to and focused on God.

The danger comes when, no
longer relying on God, you neglect
to focus your eyes on Him.

The Secret of Spiritual Consistency

God forbid that I should boast except in the cross of our Lord Jesus Christ.
(Galatians 6:14)

Paul could let his external life change without internal distress because he was rooted and grounded in God.

In secular history the Cross is an infinitesimally small thing, but from the biblical perspective it is of more importance than all the empires of the world.

The Focal Point of Spiritual Power

. . . except in the cross of our Lord Jesus Christ. (Galatians 6:14)

We have to focus on the great point of spiritual power—the Cross.

One reason for the church's feebleness is that there has not been this focus on the true center of spiritual power.

NOVEMBER 26 _____

The Consecration of Spiritual Power

. . . by whom the world has been crucified to me, and I to the world.
(Galatians 6:14)

The kind of religious life we see around the world today is entirely different from the vigorous holiness of the life of Jesus Christ.

Jesus was so much in the common everyday world that the religious people of His day accused Him of being a glutton and a drunkard.

The Riches of the Destitute

Being justified freely by His grace.
(Romans 3:24)

The greatest spiritual blessing we receive is when we come to the knowledge that we are destitute.

As long as we are "rich," particularly in the area of pride or independence, God can do nothing for us.

The Supremacy of Christ

"He will glorify Me." (John 16:14)

The holiness movements of to-day have none of the rugged re-ality of the New Testament about them.

The New Testament example of the Christian experience is that of a personal, passionate devotion to the Person of Jesus Christ.

"By the Grace of God I Am What I Am"

By the grace of God I am what I am, and His grace toward me was not in vain. (First Corinthians 15:10)

The way we continually talk about our own inabilities is an insult to our Creator.

Always be humble before God, and allow Him to be your all in all.

December

The Law and the Gospel

Whoever shall keep the whole law, and yet stumble in one point, he is guilty of all. (James 2:10)

Until a person gets there and sees that there is no hope, the Cross of Christ remains absurd to him.

When we deliberately choose to obey Him, He will reach to the remotest star and to the ends of the earth to assist us with all of His almighty power.

DECEMBER 1

Christian Perfection

*Not that I have already attained, or
am already perfected.*
(Philippians 3:12)

It is a trap to presume that God
wants to make us perfect speci-
mens of what He can do—God's purpose is to make us one with Himself.
Christian perfection is not, and
never can be, human perfection.

"Not by Might Nor by Power"

My speech and my preaching were not with persuasive words of human wisdom, but in demonstration of the Spirit and power.
(First Corinthians 2:4)

If your faith is in experiences, anything that happens is likely to upset that faith.

I must deliberately give my sanctified life to God for His service, so that He can use me as His hands and His feet.

DECEMBER 3

The Law of Opposition

To him who overcomes.
(Revelation 2:7)

Life without war is impossible in the natural or the supernatural realm.

Anything that does not strengthen me morally is the enemy of virtue within me.

"The Temple of the Holy Spirit"

Only in regard to the throne will I be greater than you. (Genesis 41:40)

God has given us the responsibility to rule over all "the temple of the Holy Spirit," including our thoughts and desires (First Corinthians 6:19).

We make excuses for things in ourselves, while we condemn things in the lives of others simply because we are not naturally inclined to do them.

DECEMBER 5 _____

"My Rainbow in the Cloud"

I set My rainbow in the cloud, and it shall be for the sign of the covenant between Me and the earth.
(Genesis 9:13)

It is the will of God that human beings should get into a right standing relationship with Him, and His covenants are designed for this purpose.

All the great blessings of God are finished and complete, but they are not mine until I enter into a relationship with Him on the basis of His covenant.

Repentance

*Godly sorrow produces repentance
leading to salvation.*
(Second Corinthians 7:10)

The foundation of Christianity is repentance.

If you ever cease to understand the value of repentance, you allow yourself to remain in sin.

The Impartial Power of God

By one offering He has perfected forever those who are being sanctified. (Hebrew 10:14)

We trample the blood of the Son of God underfoot if we think we are forgiven because we are sorry for our sins.

To identify with the death of Jesus Christ means that we must die to everything that was never a part of Him.

The Opposition of the Natural

Those who are Christ's have crucified the flesh with its passions and desires. (Galatians 5:24)

If we do not purposely sacrifice the natural, the supernatural can never become natural to us.

It is not a question of praying, but of sacrificing, and thereby performing His will.

The Offering of the Natural

It is written that Abraham had two sons; the one by a bondwoman, the other by a free woman.
(Galatians 4:22)

If we do not sacrifice the natural to the spiritual, the natural life will resist and defy the life of the Son of God.

God is not actively involved with our natural life as long as we continue to pamper and gratify it.

Individuality

Jesus said to His disciples, "If anyone desire to come after Me, let him deny himself." (Matthew 16:24)

Individuality is the hard outer layer surrounding the inner spiritual life.

Our individuality must be yielded to God so that our spiritual life may be brought forth into fellowship with Him.

Personality

. . . that they may be one just as We are one. (John 17:22)

There is only one Being who fully understands us, and that is our Creator.

Personality is the characteristic mark of the inner, spiritual man, just as individuality is the characteristic of the outer, natural man.

Intercessory Prayer

*. . . men always ought to pray and
not lose heart.* (Luke 18:1)

True intercession involves bringing the person, or the circumstance that seems to be crashing in
on you, before God, until you are
changed by His attitude toward that
person or circumstances.

Intercession is putting yourself in
God's place; it is having His mind
and perspective.

DECEMBER 13 _____

The Great Life

"Peace I leave with you, My peace I give to you; not as the world gives do I give to you. Let not your heart be troubled." (John 14:27)

God sends an immeasurable, deep peace; not a natural peace, "as the world gives," but the peace of Jesus.

Any problem that comes while I obey God, increases my overjoyed delight, because I know that my Father knows and cares, and I can watch and anticipate how He will unravel my problems.

_____ **DECEMBER 14**

"Approved to God"

*Be diligent to present yourself
approved to God, a worker who does
not need to be ashamed, rightly
dividing the word of truth.*
(Second Timothy 2:15)

Strive to re-express a truth of
God to yourself clearly and understandably,
and God will use that
same explanation when you share it
with someone else.

The time will come when that
very expression will become God's
wine of strength to someone else.

DECEMBER 15 _____

Wrestling Before God

Take up the whole armor of God . . .
praying always.
(Ephesians 6:13,18)

If you grab hold of God and wrestle with Him, as Jacob did, simply because He is working in a way that doesn't meet with your approval, you force Him to put you out of joint.

We don't have to fight or wrestle *with* God, but we must wrestle before God *with things*.

_____ **DECEMBER 16**

Redemption—Creating the Need It Satisfies

The natural man does not receive the things of the Spirit of God, for they are foolishness to him.
(First Corinthians 2:14)

The majority of people think of themselves as being completely moral, and have no sense of need for the gospel.

It is never the sharing of personal experiences that saves people, but the truth of redemption.

DECEMBER 17 _____

Test of Faithfulness

We know that all things work together for good to those who love God. (Romans 8:28)

It is only a faithful person who truly believes that God sovereignly controls his circumstances. God may cause our circumstances to suddenly fall apart, which may bring the realization of our unfaithfulness to Him for not recognizing that He had ordained the situation.

The Focus of Our Message

"I did not come to bring peace but a sword." (Matthew 10:34)

People want the blessing of God, but they can't stand something that pierces right through to the heart of the matter.

Jesus Christ came to "bring . . . a sword" through every kind of peace that is not based on a personal relationship with Himself.

The Right Kind of Help

"And I, if I am lifted up . . . will draw all peoples to Myself."
(John 12:32)

When you find yourself face to face with a person who is spiritually lost, remind yourself of Jesus Christ on the cross.

The calling of a New Testament worker is to expose sin and to reveal Jesus Christ as Savior.

Experience Or God's Revealed Truth?

We have received . . . the Spirit who is from God, that we might know the things that have been freely given to us by God. (First Corinthians 2:12)

My experience is not what makes redemption real—redemption is reality.

Faith based on experience is not faith; faith based on God's revealed truth is the only faith there is.

The Drawing of the Father

"No one can come to Me unless the Father who sent Me draws him."
(John 6:44)

When God speaks, never discuss it with anyone as if to decide what your response may be (see Galatians 1:15–16).

Belief is not the result of an intellectual act, but the result of an act of my will whereby I deliberately commit myself.

Sharing in the Atonement

*God forbid that I should boast except
in the cross of our Lord Jesus Christ.*
(Galatians 6:14)

Do I long to be so closely identified with Jesus that I am of no
value for anything except Him and
His purposes?

You must get alone with Jesus
and either decide to tell Him that
you do not want sin to die out in
you, or that at any cost you want to
be identified with His death.

The Hidden Life

*. . . your life is hidden with Christ
in God. (Colossians 3:3)*

The Spirit of God testifies to and confirms the simple, but almighty, security of the life that "is hidden with Christ in God."

The most dangerous and unsure thing is to try to live without God.

His Birth and Our New Birth

Behold, the virgin shall be with child, and bear a Son, and they shall call His name Immanuel, which is translated, "God with us."
(Matthew 1:23)

Jesus Christ is not the best human being the human race can boast of—He is a Being for whom the human race can take no credit at all.

The evidence of the new birth is that I yield myself so completely to God that "Christ is formed" in me.

DECEMBER 25 _____

"Walk in the Light"

If we walk in the light as He is in the light . . . the blood of Jesus Christ His Son cleanses us from all sins.
(First John 1:7)

For a person to really know what sin is requires the full work and deep touch of the atonement of Jesus Christ, that is, the imparting of His absolute perfection.

The Holy Spirit applies or administers the work of the atonement to us in the deep unconscious realm as well as in the conscious realm.

Where the Battle Is Won Or Lost

"If you will return, O Israel," says the Lord. (Jeremiah 4:1)

Our battles are first won or lost in the secret places of our will in God's presence, never in full view of the world.

Get alone with God, do battle before Him, and settle the matter once and for all.

Continuous Conversion

". . . unless you are converted and become as little children, you will by no means enter the kingdom of heaven." (Matthew 18:3)

When God through His sovereignty brings us into new situations, we should immediately make sure that our natural life submits to the spiritual, obeying the Spirit of God.

What God sees as stubborn weakness, we call strength.

_____ **DECEMBER 28**

Deserter Or Disciple?

From that time many of His disciples went back and walked with Him no more. (John 6:66)

Mentally disobeying the "heavenly vision" (Acts 26:19) will make you a slave to ideas and views that are completely foreign to Jesus Christ.

If a New Testament standard is revealed to us by the light of God, and we don't try to measure up, or even feel inclined to do so, then we begin to backslide.

DECEMBER 29 _____

"And Every Virtue We Possess"

All my springs are in you.
(Psalm 87:7)

We want to cling to our natural virtues, while all the time God is trying to get us in contact with the life of Jesus Christ.

It is the saddest thing to see people who are trying to serve God depending on that which the grace of God never gave them.

Yesterday

You shall not go out with haste, . . .
for the Lord will go before you, and
the God of Israel will be your rear
guard. (Isaiah 52:12)

At the end of the year we turn
with eagerness to all that God
has for the future, and yet anxiety is
apt to arise when we remember our
yesterdays.

God will keep watch so that we
will not be tripped up again by the
same failures, as would undoubtedly
happen if He were not our "rear
guard."

DECEMBER 31